MAY THE SPIRIT OF THE LIVING GOD SPEAK TO YOU THROUGH THIS BOOK.

Presented to:

_____

by:

_____

Date:

_____

"...THE TRUTH WILL SET YOU FREE." (JOHN 8:32 - ESV)

God wants to be your father

GOD WANTS TO BE YOUR FATHER

C. Orville McLeish

---
*God wants you to know He loves you,
and desires greatly to be your "Daddy."*

GOD WANTS TO BE YOUR FATHER

ISBN-13: 978-1-953759-22-1 (paperback)
ISBN-13: 978-1-953759-23-8 (hardback)
ISBN-13: 978-1-953759-24-5 (eBook)

Copyright © 2014 by C. Orville McLeish

All rights reserved solely by the author. No part of this book may be reproduced, stored in a retrieval system or transmitted by any means without the written permission of the author.

Unless otherwise states, all quotations are taken from the HOLY BIBLE, NEW LIVING TRANSLATION, copyright 1996, 2004, 2007 by the Tyndale House Foundation. Used by permission of Tyndale House Publishers Inc., Carol Stream, IL 30188. All rights reserved.

Scripture quotations marked as KJV are from the HOLY BIBLE, KING JAMES VERSION, © 1972, 1976, 1979, 1983, 1984, 1985 Thomas Nelson Inc.

Scripture quotations noted AMP are from the Amplified Bible, © 1972, 1976, 1979, 1983, 1984, 1985 Thomas Nelson Inc. All rights reserved. Used by permission.

Scripture quotation noted NASB are from the New American Standard Bible ®, © Copyright the Lockman Foundation 1960, 1963, 1963, 1968, 1971, 1972, 1973, 1975, 1977. All rights reserved. Used by permission.

Scripture taken from The Message. Copyright 1993, 1994, 1995, 1996, 2000, 2001, 2002. Used by permission of NavPress Publishing Group.

This book is dedicated to the memory of my earthly father, Percival Wilfred McLeish. (1931 – 2012).

CONTENTS

Introduction 11
1 Our Father on Earth 15
2 Our Father in Heaven 25
3 Dear Atheist 33
4 Dear Wayward Son 39
5 Dear Double Minded Man 59
6 Dear Backslider, Come Home 71
7 Dear Confused Mind 93
8 The Father Has Given You His Kingdom 109
9 God's Adoption Plan 129

INTRODUCTION

Percival Wilfred McLeish breathed his last breath, and his spirit left his body in September 2012. Being in the same room with death was haunting, and the initial effect lasted for months. Even today, that moment replays in my head.

After he died, I came by his bed several times just to look at him during the "processing" before the mortician came on the scene. It was a surreal moment. My father looked like he was sleeping, but he was dead. Whatever possessed his body, enabling him to roll his eyes or move his limbs was no longer present in his mortal body. Who took it? Where did it go? Can it possibly return in that very moment? None of us had any control over what transpired, it seems.

My father would never be able to move by himself in this life ever again. His body had to be carried to the morgue, dressed, placed in a casket (not of his choosing), taken to a church, and then taken to a plot of land to be buried. He could no longer do this for himself. This was a stark reality and the expected end of us all, but it should sensitize us to a new reality. There must be more to us than a physical body. There is an essence that radiates all around us that enables us to live, move, and breathe and be aware of our surroundings. "For in Him, we live and move and exist." (Acts 17:28 - NLT).

We say there is no God while simultaneously ignoring the true fact that we cannot even explain our own existence.

How do we live in water for nine months before we are born, yet, after birth, we cannot last nine minutes under water. It takes just thirty seconds to drown. Do you really think it is easier to believe God? The Bible says, "I knew you before I formed you in your mother's womb . . ." (Jeremiah 1:5 - NLT).

So death happens when our physical body loses its natural function. I knew my father was dying, but I could not understand "how" he was dying. Fact is, when our organs fail to function as they should, the essence of life or spirit/soul has to abandon its host and return to God.

I heard someone say once, it is easier to believe there is no God than to believe that there is. I am inclined to disagree. I always knew there was a God. The awareness of that fact was evident from as far back as I can remember. It made perfect sense as a child, then a teen, young adult, and adult. I do not question it. I accept it. Did that awareness stop me from sinning? It did not. But my sins never changed who God is, nor did it affect in any way His love for me. He died for me as a wretched sinner. If I am a Christian who sins, then His love would be just as strong. But knowing about God's love, and living in His love, is not the same thing.

This brings us to the whole point of writing this book. I had a serious problem believing or accepting that I could have this relationship with God. I struggled with this for a very long time. It made no sense to me. How can mortal have a relationship with Invisible? I could never fully grasp the idea of what it meant to be a "child of God" until my latter years.

I am now cognizant of the fact that God desires to have this close, intimate relationship with everyone—including you! God wants to be your Father.

My vision for this book is really a simple one. I have known many who died without Christ. I am seeing some of my family members on that road of sin and destruction, and I cannot seem to do anything about it. One night, I complained to God and told Him it was easier for me to write than to talk. So, He said I should write them a letter. That thought has evolved into this book. Each chapter is as much God's letter to you as they are mine as they reveal His heart towards us.

The vision is really answering the question, "If Jesus walked this earth today, as He did so many centuries ago, what would He be saying to you as He meets you along the way?" We both know that Jesus still walks the earth (the Holy Spirit), but those we address might not be able to relate to this fact as those of us who have had a genuine experience with God.

The message is so simple, "God wants to be your Father!"

1

OUR FATHER ON EARTH

GOOD OR BAD, PRESENT OR passive, a dad defines us. He shapes what we become, how we think, how we act, how we feel about ourselves, and how we respond to others. We develop so much of our first emotions and feelings by his words and actions. The way fathers behave—what was said to you, how you were treated, everything he did and did not do—impacted you somehow. Depending on how you were cared for, mistreated, or just plain ignored, you have come up with your own ideas of what a father is like. Because of this, I am quite certain that how you see and perceive your heavenly Father, God, has also been impacted—distorted even—by your relationship with your earthly dad.

We hear stories all the time of people who feel abandoned, devalued, criticized, and unable to measure up. Stories of horrible abusive dads who were there but, in reality, were never really "there," has shaped the future of tomorrow's fathers. Yet, as important as a dad is, many children throughout Western civilization are living without a father, or they bear the scars of an abusive, demanding, uninvolved father. The statistics are frightening:

- 63 percent of youth suicide victims are from

fatherless homes.

- 90 percent of all homeless and runaway children are from fatherless homes.

- 80 percent of rapists with anger problems come from fatherless homes.

- 71 percent of all high-school dropouts come from fatherless homes.

- Children living in two-parent households with a poor relationship with their father are 68 percent more likely to smoke, drink, or use drugs, compared to all teens in two-parent households.

- Children with fathers who are involved are 40 percent less likely to repeat a grade in school.

- Adolescent girls raised in two-parent homes with involved fathers are significantly less likely to be sexually active than girls raised without involved fathers.

Compared to living with both parents, living in a single-parent home doubles the risk that a child will suffer physical, emotional, or educational neglect. The overall rate of child abuse and neglect in single-parent households is 27.3 children per 1,000, whereas the rate of overall maltreatment in two-parent households is 15.5 per 1,000.

Daughters of single parents without a father involved are 53% more likely to marry as teenagers, 71% more likely to have children as teenagers, 64% more likely to have a pre-marital birth, and 92% more likely to get divorced themselves.

Adolescent girls raised in a two-parent home with involved fathers are significantly less likely to be sexually active than girls raised without involved fathers.

These statistics point to an epidemic rather than just a problem, and they cannot be ignored. As a result, the signs in recent decades, which demonstrate the deterioration of family and social life in the United States, for example, are startling. One indication of our nation's demise is the spiritual decline and the increased number of young people being reared by mothers without the benefit of a father.

Even when the father is present, he is often fully negligent, focusing upon a demanding job and career. His influence over a family's daily affairs often would not even be noticed except for the paycheck he provides. The generic modern father is often remote, indifferent, unapproachable, and unavailable. He is a member of a misunderstood endangered species known as "father."

Psychologists say that a child's basic personality and unique responsiveness to his environment are established in the first five years of life. The age of gender identity formation may occur even earlier. Should not the role of the father extend beyond the mere initiation of life when the sperm is furnished to fertilize an egg?

It is commonly acknowledged that children need to receive affection, affirmation, discipline, and instruction from both parents. We are more influenced both positively and negatively during childhood and adolescence by adult role models than our peers influence us. A caring father who nourishes an intimate and loving relationship has a profound effect on a child's life. Children need caring and loving fathers.

It is not always a mother's fault that her husband is not there. If she seeks God's help and mercy, her children can often be headed into a path of wholeness and godlikeness in spite of a missing father. Many individuals have come from broken homes or difficult family backgrounds and yet experience fullness and wholeness. Many of these individuals take special care to make sure their own sons and daughters are reared in a loving and balanced family environment.

What if God was a bigger version of your dad? Would He leave you when you fail? Or would He punish you for not measuring up? So many people wrestle with the concept of God as Father. A. W. Tozer said, "What comes into our minds when we think about God is the most important thing about us."[1] Why? Because how we see God determines how we relate to God, and how we relate to God determines everything else about us. We will never become all we were intended to be until we can see God for who He is, not whom we imagined Him to be.

Consider just a few ways in which your image of your father possibly may have affected your perception of God, which in turn affects your self-image. If your father was distant, impersonal, and uncaring, and he would not intervene for you, you may see God as having the same characteristics. As a result, you feel that you are unworthy of God's intervention in your life. You find it difficult to draw close to God because you see Him as disinterested in your need and wants.

---

[1] http://www.goodreads.com/quotes/376518-what-comes-into-our-minds-when-we-think-about-god

If your father was a pushy man who was inconsiderate of you or violated and used you, you might see God in the same way. You probably feel cheap or worthless in God's eyes and perhaps feel that you deserve to be taken advantage of by others. You may feel that God will force you—not ask you—to do things you do not want to do.

If your father was like a drill sergeant, demanding more and more from you with no expression of satisfaction or burning with anger with no tolerance for mistakes, you might have cast God in his image. You likely feel that God will not accept you unless you meet His demands, which seem unattainable. This perception may have driven you to become a perfectionist.

If your father was a weakling, and you could not depend on him to help you or defend you, your image of God may be that of a weakling. You may feel that you are unworthy of God's comfort and support or that He is unable to help you.

If your father was overly critical and constantly came down on you, or if he did not believe in you or your capabilities and discouraged you from trying, you may perceive God in the same way. You do not feel as if you are worth God's respect or trust. You may even see yourself as a continual failure, deserving all the criticism you receive.

In contrast to the negative perceptions many women have about God, let me give you several positive character qualities of a father. Notice how these qualities, if they existed in your father, have positively influenced your perception of God.

If your father was patient, you are more likely to see God as patient and available for you. You feel that you are worth God's time and concern. You feel important to God and that He is personally involved in every aspect of your life.

If your father was kind, you probably see God acting kindly and graciously on your behalf. You feel that you are worth God's help and intervention. You feel God's love for you deeply, and you are convinced that He wants to relate to you personally.

If your father was a giving man, you might perceive God as someone who gives to you and supports you. You feel that you are worth God's support and encouragement. You believe that God will give you what is best for you, and you respond by giving of yourself to others.

If your father accepted you, you tend to see God accepting you regardless of what you do. God does not dump on you or reject you when you struggle but understands and encourages you. You are able to accept yourself even when you blow it or do not perform up to your potential.

If your father protected you, you probably perceive God as your protector in life. You feel that you are worthy of being under His care, and you rest in His security.

Try it—think about God right now. What comes into your mind? What feelings or images come to you? What does He "look" like to you? How do you think He feels about you? Be honest here—do not give some churchy answer that you think you are supposed to give if that is not what you really feel deep inside of your heart.

When you think of your earthly father, what is the first thing that comes into your mind? Jokester? Provider? Teacher? Generous? Or do you think of abandonment, abuse, or neglect? Maybe you think passive, uninterested, or controlling and judgmental. Some of you will be thinking of a dad who expected more than you could ever give or more than you could ever be. Today, there are successful businesspersons and church leaders—who are still trying to please that kind of father. Perhaps your father loved you but never disciplined you. Or maybe your dad was loving and amazing.

Regardless of your answer, or whatever comes to mind when you think about your father, there is a good chance that you attribute similar characteristics to your image of your heavenly Father. Simply put, your image of God has been formed and shaped by the father figures in your life.

The distortion of how we see God ultimately comes from what the Bible refers to as our enemy, the devil, satan. Satan is a liar who wants to distort, discredit, and deceive you about God the Father. Satan is not just a liar but also *"the father of lies"* (See John 8:44), and his number-one goal is to deceive you by making God out to be less than He is. Deception is the primary tool satan uses to misdirect your attention away from a God who is madly in love with you, sent His Son, and died in your place so that you have the opportunity to live with Him in heaven forever.

Some of you would say you have no desire for a relationship with God. Your image of God may be so distorted you have nixed the possibility of forming any kind of connection with Him. After ready this book, I hope that your image of God will be clearer and brighter than it is right now and that your relationship with Him would be stronger. God has revealed Himself through His creation, and you can see evidence of Him all around. He has also revealed Himself in each of our hearts. The Bible tells us in Ecclesiastes 3:11, *"Yet God has made everything beautiful for its own time. He has planted eternity in the human heart, but even so, people cannot see the whole scope of God's work from beginning to end."*

A WORD OF THOUGHT

"Pray like this: Our Father in heaven, may your name be kept holy." (Matthew 6:9)

"Everyone who acknowledges me publicly here on earth, I will also acknowledge before my Father in heaven." (Matthew 10:32)

"I also tell you this: If two of you agree here on earth concerning anything you ask, my Father in heaven will do it for you." (Matthew 18:19)

"All praise to God, the Father of our Lord Jesus Christ, who has blessed us with every spiritual blessing in the heavenly realms because we are united with Christ." (Ephesians 1:3)

"Are we not all children of the same Father? Are we not all created by the same God? Then why do we betray each other, violating the covenant of our ancestors?" (Malachi 2:10)

"Father to the fatherless, defender of widows—this is God, whose dwelling is holy." (Psalm 68:5)

"At that same time Jesus was filled with the joy of the Holy Spirit, and he said, "O Father, Lord of heaven and earth, thank you for hiding these things from those who think themselves wise and clever, and for revealing them to the childlike. Yes, Father, it pleased you to do it this way. My Father has entrusted everything to me. No one truly knows the Son except the Father, and no one truly knows the Father except the Son and those to whom the Son chooses to reveal him." (Luke 10:21-22)

2

OUR FATHER IN HEAVEN

IN SCRIPTURE THERE ARE MANY different names used to describe God and portray Him. We could portray God as a faithful companion and a true comrade. We could emphasize certain Biblical texts that would show God as one's "best friend." We examine a variety of songs that make us think of God as a warm, fuzzy, close, and cuddly teddy bear. However, it is essential to present God as He revealed Himself in Scripture.

When God presented Himself to Moses, He told him, *"I am who I am"* (See Exodus 2:14), but what does that mean? A close examination of God's Word, we can discover who God is by the revelation of a variety of names of God.

First, we have Elohim (translated "God" in the English Bible). Elohim existed before creation. It is a Hebrew name used for God in the very first verse of the Bible. Elohim is a plural noun, which in pagan cultures refers to various gods, or human authorities of the nations. The Bible, however, uses this noun to refer to the one true God. Most theologians agree that the inspired author used this plural version as an early hint that later would reveal the fact that He is one God in nature and purpose, but is revealed as one God in three persons, the Trinity.

Next, we have El, or El-Shaddai. The word El emphasizes the power of God and Shaddai His sovereignty. Combined, it is literally translated, "Mighty . . . Mighty God," so collectively it is translated, "Almighty God." This is the name God revealed when He made a covenant relationship with Abraham (See Genesis 17:1-2).

Another name not used by most believers is the most personal name God gives Himself in the Old Testament; it is Yahweh. In the Hebrew language, it originally did not use vowels. Instead, each constant carried a vowel sound according to its placement and structure in a word or sentence. Yahweh was spelled YHWH.

Five hundred years after the death of Christ, a group of Jews called the Massoretes developed a vowel system to ensure the phonic sounds would remain true to its origin. YHWH was considered so holy, that when scribes translated the word, they added the vowels, which changed the pronunciation of Yahweh to Jehovah. In addition, it was so holy that when read, the reader would say, Adonai, and not Yahweh.

Most English translations translate Yahweh as "LORD" (in all caps), and when it is the Hebrew word Adonai, they translate it "Lord." Such as, *"I saw the Lord (Adonai) seated on a throne"* (Isaiah 6:1). Historically, the word Yahweh is directly tied to covenant language. Therefore, the development from Elohim and El-Shaddai, a powerful God, shifted to Yahweh, a personal, intimate, loving, and covenant-keeping God.

Two hundred fifty years before Christ, the Greek language was forced upon the Jews during the captivity of the Greeks under the leadership of Alexander the Great. With a widespread international language (Greek), the scribes translated the Hebrew Bible into Greek, called the Septuagint. When doing so, the translators used the word "Theos," which is a Greek word for God, where we got the word Theology (Theos – God and ology – (logos), meaning "word" or "research," thus translated to mean, the study of God).

Now, the Old Testament described God (Pater in Greek) as the Father of His people in numerous places (Deuteronomy 32:6, Isaiah 63:16, 64:8), but Jesus promoted this name of God to a much higher level of importance. Jesus considered God His own Father (Pater) and the Father of His disciples, whom He instructed to pray to "Our Father."

While all the names of God are important in many ways, the name "Abba Father" is one of the most significant names of God in understanding how He relates to people. Recent scholarship has shown that, although the New Testament was written in Greek, the main language that Jesus and His disciples spoke was undoubtedly Aramaic, an ancient regional language. The Aramaic word *Abba* appears three times in the New Testament (See Mark 14:36, Romans 8:15, Galatians 4:6), and each time it is immediately translated as *Pater* for readers unfamiliar with Aramaic. It seems that when Jesus spoke of God as Father in Aramaic, he used the term *Abba*. It is particularly remarkable, then, that *Abba* is an intimate word for father. It indicates some of the very first syllables a baby might pronounce in reference to his father – something like Daddy or Papa, but even more like Dada.

The word *Abba* is an Aramaic word that would most closely be translated as "Daddy." It was a common term that young children would use to address their fathers. It signifies the close, intimate relationship of a father to his child, as well as the childlike trust that a young child puts in his "daddy."

While most people, at least those who do not deny God's existence, would claim that all are "children of God," the Bible reveals quite a different truth. We are all His creations and under His authority and Lordship and will all be judged by Him, but being a child of God and having the right to truly call Him "Abba Father" is something that only born-again Christians are able to do (See John 1:12-13).

Understanding that not all people are children of God and that becoming a child of God only happens when you are adopted by God through faith in Christ Jesus (See Galatians 3:26) is important for understanding how and why God deals with people differently. If we are born again (See John 1:12, 3:1-8), we have been adopted into the family of God, redeemed from the curse of sin, and are "joint-heirs with Christ Jesus" (See Romans 8:17, Galatians 4:7). Part of that new relationship is that God now deals with us differently, which includes His chastisement when we sin (See Hebrews 12:3-11). Because of that new relationship, Christians may sin, but they cannot be comfortable or content living a life of habitual, ongoing sin. If people are living a life enslaved to sin and are comfortable in that sin and without the chastisement of God upon them, then we know they are "illegitimate and not sons" (See Hebrews 12:8). In other words, they are unbelievers.

The misguided but popular concept that all people are children of God and can truthfully call Him "Abba Father" is simply not true. Just as children do not choose to be adopted or choose who will adopt them, neither do

Christians choose to become children of God. Instead, God chooses them. He predestines them "to adoption as sons by Jesus Christ to Himself, according to the good pleasure of His will" (Ephesians 1:5), having been chosen by God from "before the foundation of the world" (See Ephesians 1:4).

To be adopted by God means that we are accepted into His family, and this brings a multitude of blessings and responsibilities. Christians are legally adopted as sons into God's family. Paul uses the term "adopted as sons" to write to the believers in Rome, where they would have understood this in a specific context. Under Roman law, if you were an adopted son, you had identical legal rights to a son born naturally in the family. An adopted son had the right to the family name of the person who adopted him and the right to an inheritance of the father's property. *"Wherefore thou art no more a servant, but a son; and if a son, then an heir of God through Christ."* (Galatians 4:7).

For us, this means that we have been given the name of Christ and have the right to be called Christians. Our inheritance is nothing less than the property of our Heavenly Father—all the spiritual riches that are in Christ, both in the present life and in our life to come.

Under Roman law, the adopted son also had the right to the father's citizenship of the Empire. We also obtained a new citizenship when our Father adopted us, and we have become *citizens of heaven*—our true home. The father who adopts was also granted full rights and responsibilities of a natural father—he had complete authority over the adopted son and also had the legal role of caregiver. With full, loving authority over us, our Father has accepted His responsibility to care for us, and He has the right, and desire, to correct us when we are wrong and to discipline us when we step out of line.

Our Father God is infinitely patient, wise, and loving, and the Bible tells us that the fact that God *does* discipline us is proof in itself that we have been adopted into His family.

As we come to understand the true nature of God as revealed in the Bible, we should be amazed that He not only allows us, but also He even encourages us, to call Him, "Abba Father." It is amazing that a holy and righteous God, who created and sustains all things, who is the only all-powerful, all-knowing, ever-present God, would allow sinful humans to call Him "Daddy." As we come to understand who God really is and how sinful we are, the privilege of being able to call Him "Abba Father" will take on a completely new meaning for us and help us understand God's amazing grace.

It is life-changing to understand the full force of what it means to be able to call the one true God our "Daddy" and what it means to be joint-heirs with Christ. Because of our relationship with God, we know He no longer deals with us as enemies. Instead, we can approach a holy God as our heavenly Father with "boldness" (See Hebrews 11:19) and "full assurance of faith" (See Hebrews 11:22). We have that confidence because of the indwelling presence of the Holy Spirit who *"bears witness with our spirit that we are children of God, and if children, then heirs—heirs of God and joint-heirs with Christ, if indeed we suffer with Him, that we may also be glorified together."* (Romans 8:16-17).

The benefits of being adopted children of God are many. Becoming a child of God is the highest privilege and honor that can be imagined. Because of it, we have a new relationship with God and a new standing before Him. He deals with His children differently than He deals with the rest of the world. Being a child of God, adopted "through faith in Christ Jesus" is the source for our hope, the security of our future, and the motivation to *"walk worthy of the calling with which you were called"* (Ephesians 4:1). Being children of the King of kings and Lord of lords calls us to a higher standard, a different way of life, and a greater hope.

A WORD OF THOUGHT

"Jesus said, 'This is how you should pray: Father, may your name be kept holy. May your Kingdom come soon.'" (Luke 11:2)

"So you have not received a spirit that makes you fearful slaves. Instead, you received God's Spirit when he adopted you as his own children. Now we call him, 'Abba, Father.'" (Romans 8:15)

"And because we are his children, God has sent the Spirit of his Son into our hearts, prompting us to call out, 'Abba, Father.'" (Galatians 4:6)

"Abba, Father," he cried out, "everything is possible for you. Please take this cup of suffering away from me. Yet I want your will to be done, not mine." (Mark 14:36)

3

DEAR ATHEIST

CAN SOMEONE REALLY SAY THERE is no God? In reality, even if we go through our entire lives and never see anything supernatural, a miracle, healing, or signs and wonders...there is evidence enough that points to the reality of God's existence. I want to explore this in-depth.

When it comes to the possibility of God's existence, the Bible says that there are people who have seen sufficient evidence, but they have suppressed the truth about God (Romans 1:19-21). On the other hand, for those who want to know God, if He is there, He says, *"You will seek me and find me; when you seek me with all your heart, I will be found by you."* (Jeremiah 29:13-14). Before you look at the facts surrounding God's existence, ask yourself, "If God does exist, would I want to know him?" Here then, are some reasons to consider.

The complexity of our planet points to a deliberate Designer who not only created our universe but also sustains it today. Many examples showing God's design could be given, possibly with no end. For instance, the earth—its size is perfect. The earth's size and corresponding gravity hold a thin layer of mostly nitrogen and oxygen gases, only extending about 50 miles above the earth's surface. If earth were smaller, an atmosphere would be impossible, like the planet Mercury. If earth were larger, its atmosphere would contain free hydrogen, like Jupiter.[2] Earth is the only known planet equipped with an atmosphere of the right mixture of gases to sustain plant, animal, and human life.

The earth is located the right distance from the sun. Consider the temperature swings we encounter, roughly -30 degrees to +120 degrees. If the earth were any further away from the sun, we would all freeze. Any closer and we would burn up. Even a fractional variance in the earth's position to the sun would make life on earth impossible. The earth remains this perfect distance from the sun while it rotates around the sun at a speed of nearly 67,000 mph. It is also rotating on its axis, allowing the earth's entire surface to be properly warmed and cooled every day.

In addition, our moon is the perfect size and distance from the earth for its gravitational pull. The moon creates important ocean tides and movement, so ocean waters do not stagnate, and yet our massive oceans are restrained from spilling over across the continents.[3]

Another example is the human brain that simultaneously processes an amazing amount of information. Your brain takes in all the colors and objects you see, such as the temperature around you, the pressure of your feet against the floor, the sounds around you, the dryness of your mouth, even the texture of your keyboard. Your brain holds and processes all your emotions, thoughts, and memories. At the same time, your brain keeps track of

---

[2] R.E.D. Clark, *Creation* (London: Tyndale Press, 1946), p. 20
[3] The Wonders of God's Creation, Moody Institute of Science (Chicago, IL)

the ongoing functions of your body like your breathing pattern, eyelid movement, hunger and movement of the muscles in your hands—the human brain processes more than a million messages a second.[4] Your brain weighs the importance of all this data, filtering out the relatively unimportant. This screening function is what allows you to focus and operate effectively in your world. The brain functions differently than other organs. There is intelligence to it, the ability to reason, produce feelings, dream and plan, take action, and relate to other people.

We all agree the universe had a start, but what caused it? Scientists are convinced that our universe began with one enormous explosion of energy and light, which we now call the Big Bang. This was the singular start to everything that exists: the beginning of the universe, the start of space, and even the initial start of time itself. Christians believe that an enormous explosion of energy and light is what one would expect if a Supreme Being spoke the world into existence.

Astrophysicist Robert Jastrow, a self-described agnostic, stated, "The seed of everything that has happened in the universe was planted in that first instant; every star, every planet and every living creature in the universe came into being as a result of events that were set in motion in the moment of the cosmic explosion. The universe flashed into being, and we cannot find out what caused that to happen."[5]

Steven Weinberg, a Nobel laureate in Physics, said at

---

[4] Ibid.
[5] Robert Jastrow, "Message from Professor Robert Jastrow"; *LeaderU.com;* 2002.

the moment of this explosion, "the universe was about a hundred thousand million degrees centigrade...and the universe was filled with light."[6] *"And God said, 'Let there be light . . .'"* (Genesis 1:3 - KJV).

The universe has not always existed. It had a start. What caused that? Scientists have no explanation for the sudden explosion of light and matter, but the Bible does.

The universe operates by uniform laws of nature. Why does it? Much of life may seem uncertain, but look at what we can count on day after day: gravity remains consistent, a hot cup of coffee left on a counter will get cold, the earth rotates in the same 24 hours, and the speed of light does not change—on earth or in galaxies far from us.

How is it that we can identify laws of nature that *never* change? Why is the universe so orderly, so reliable? "The greatest scientists have been struck by how strange this is. There is no logical necessity for a universe that obeys rules, let alone one that abides by the rules of mathematics. This astonishment springs from the recognition that the universe does not have to behave this way. It is easy to imagine a universe in which conditions change unpredictably from instant to instant, or even a universe in which things pop in and out of existence."[7] Richard Feynman, a Nobel Prize winner for quantum electrodynamics, said, "Why nature is mathematical is a mystery. The fact that there are rules at all is a kind of miracle."[8]

---

[6] Steven Weinberg; *The First Three Minutes: A Modern View of the Origin of the Universe;* (Basic Books,1988); p 5.

[7] Dinesh D'Souza, *What's So Great about Christianity;* (Regnery Publishing, Inc, 2007, chapter 11).

[8] Richard Feynman, *The Meaning of It All: Thoughts of a Citizen-Scientist* (New York: BasicBooks, 1998), 43.

It is easier to believe that there is no God than try to substitute a claim that there is no God. The choice to believe has always been yours, but know that this same God has a strong insatiable desire to be your Father.

A WORD OF THOUGHT

"Only fools say in their hearts, "There is no God." They are corrupt, and their actions are evil; not one of them does good!" (Psalm 14:1)

"So you have not received a spirit that makes you fearful slaves. Instead, you received God's Spirit when he adopted you as his own children. Now we call him, 'Abba, Father.'" (Romans 8:15)

"And because we are his children, God has sent the Spirit of his Son into our hearts, prompting us to call out, 'Abba, Father.'" (Galatians 4:6)

"Abba, Father," he cried out, "everything is possible for you. Please take this cup of suffering away from me. Yet I want your will to be done, not mine." (Mark 14:36)

4

DEAR WAYWARD SON

WHEN ADAM AND EVE SINNED in the Garden of Eden (paradise), they fell from grace. In a sense, God tested humanity, and we failed. Nevertheless, why did Adam and Eve need to be in paradise to be tested? It is because they were in an unfallen state, and so it was fitting for them to be in an unfallen place. They did not fall because a fallen creation surrounded them, but because free will choose badly when tempted.

God warned Adam from the beginning, *"But the* LORD *God warned him, "You may freely eat the fruit of every tree in the garden—except the tree of the knowledge of good and evil. If you eat its fruit, you are sure to die."* (Genesis 2:17). The parable of the Garden of Eden focuses on the first sin of Adam and Eve. The Garden of Eden contained two special trees. The first was the forbidden tree of knowledge of good and evil, and the second tree was the tree of everlasting life.

The Genesis story tells us that Adam and Eve disobeyed God's commandment and fell into sin under the temptations of satan. They freely chose to defy God by eating from the forbidden tree of good and evil. The Church teaches us that this first sin of man constituted a loss of trust in man for God and an abuse of humanity's freedom. Because man had disobeyed their Creator and indulged in sin, man finally knew of evil and lost his original justice and holiness. Man's privileged and harmonious state in the Garden of Eden was torn asunder, and devastating results ensued. For the first time, death entered into the world, and man was doomed to experience a terminal nature. *"By the sweat of your brow will you have food to eat until you return to the ground from which you were made. For you were made from dust, and to dust you will return."* (Genesis 3:19). Women received the pangs of childbirth and were placed under the dominion of man, *"I will sharpen the pain of your pregnancy, and in pain you will give birth. And you will desire to control your husband, but he will rule over you."* (Genesis 3:16).

Finally, nature turned against man, *"Since you listened to your wife and ate from the tree whose fruit I commanded you not to eat the ground is cursed because of you. All your life you will struggle to scratch a living from it. It will grow thorns and thistles for you, though you will eat of its grains."* (Genesis 3:17-18).

Adam's sin brought devastating consequences, death, and the upset of the harmonious balance between God, man, and creation. In addition, the will of man is forever weakened by the first sin. Original sin, the loss of original justice and holiness, affected the offspring of Adam and Eve through weakness of will. No longer does humanity safe haven original justice and holiness but is instead drawn toward evil and selfish pleasures. We call this weakness of the will *concupiscence*. The continuing temptations of satan and the loss of the gifts of original holiness and justice marred the soul of Adam, and as he is the head of the human race, all of his descendants were likewise convicted. The stain of original sin is inherited by all humans at the moment of conception and brings its effects of ignorance, concupiscence, death, and suffering.

So then, how did the Fall affect humanity? The Bible says, *"When Adam sinned, sin entered the world. Adam's sin brought death, so death spread to everyone, for everyone sinned."* (Romans 5:12). The effects of the Fall are numerous and far-reaching. Sin has affected every aspect of our being. It has affected our lives on earth and our eternal destiny.

One of the immediate effects of the Fall was that mankind was separated from God. In the Garden of Eden, Adam and Eve had perfect communion and fellowship with God. When they rebelled against Him, that fellowship was broken. They became aware of their sin and were ashamed before Him. They hid from Him (See Genesis 3:8-10), and man has been hiding from God ever since. Only through Christ can that fellowship be restored, because in Him we are made as righteous and sinless in God's eyes as Adam and Eve were before they sinned. *"For God made Christ, who never sinned, to be the offering for our sin, so that we could be made right with God through Christ."* (2 Corinthians 5:21).

Because of the Fall, death became a reality, and all creation was subject to it. All men die; all animals die, all plant life dies. The *"whole creation groans"* (See Romans 8:22), waiting for the time when Christ will return to liberate it from the effects of death. Because of sin, death is an inescapable reality, and no one is immune. *"For the wages of sin is death, but the gift of God is eternal life in*

Christ Jesus our Lord." (Romans 6:23 - KJV). Worse still, we not only die, but if we die without Christ, we experience eternal death.

Another effect of the Fall is that humans have lost sight of the purpose for which they were created. Man's chief end and highest purpose in life is to glorify God and enjoy Him forever (See Romans 11:36; 1 Corinthians 6:20; 1 Corinthians 10:31; Psalm 86:9). For this reason, love for God is the core of all morality and goodness. The opposite is the choice of self as supreme. Selfishness is the real meaning of the Fall of Man, and what follows are all other crimes against God. In all ways, sin is a turning in upon oneself, which is confirmed in how we live our lives. We call attention to ourselves and to our good qualities and accomplishments. We minimize our shortcomings. We seek special favors and opportunities in life, wanting an extra edge that no one else has. We display vigilance to our own wants and needs, while we ignore those of others. In short, we place ourselves upon the throne of our lives, usurping God's role.

When Adam chose to rebel against his Creator, he lost his innocence, incurred the penalty of physical and spiritual death, and his mind was darkened by sin, as are the minds of his successors. The apostle Paul said of pagans, *"Since they thought it foolish to acknowledge God, he abandoned them to their foolish thinking and let them do things that should never be done."* (Romans 1:28). He told the Corinthians, *"the god of this age has blinded the minds of unbelievers so that they cannot see the light of the Gospel of the glory of Christ, who is the image of God."* (2 Corinthians 4:4 - KJV). Jesus said, *"I have come into the world as a light so that no one who believes in me should stay in darkness."* (John 12:46 - KJV). Paul reminded the Ephesians, *"For once you were full of darkness, but now you have light from the Lord. So live as people of light!"* (Ephesians 5:8). The purpose of salvation is *"to open their eyes, so they may turn from darkness to light and from the power of Satan to God. Then they will receive forgiveness for their sins and be given a place among God's people, who are set apart by faith in me."* (Acts 26:18).

The Fall produced in humans a state of depravity. Paul spoke of those "whose consciences are seared" (See 1 Timothy 4:2 - KJV) and those whose minds are spiritually darkened because of rejecting the truth (See Romans 1:21). In this state, man is utterly incapable of doing or choosing that which is acceptable to God, apart from divine grace. *"For the sinful nature is always hostile to God. It never did obey God's laws, and it never will."* (Romans 8:7).

The Hebrew word for temptation is "nasah." It signifies a test to prove the quality of something. It is sometimes used to denote "squeezing." Tests are not bad things. We test all kinds of products for safety purposes. We take tests to receive qualifications. We can be certain that all spiritual tests are for our benefit, but it depends upon how we respond to them.

The Hebrew word for sin is "chata." It means "to miss the mark or go astray." Spiritually it means that we do not come up to God's standards of holiness and righteousness.

The Scriptures reveal this very clearly. *"All we like sheep have gone astray; we have turned every one to his own way; and the LORD hath laid on him the iniquity of us all."* (Isaiah 53:6 - KJV). *"And he that doubteth is damned if he eat, because he eateth not of faith: for whatsoever is not of faith is sin."* (Romans 14:23 - KJV). *"Remember, it is sin to know what you ought to do and then not do it."* (James 4:17 - KJV). *"Whosoever committeth sin transgresseth also the law: for sin is the transgression of the law."* (1 John 4:3 - KJV)

Therefore, sin is following the temptation to disobey God, to act wickedly, or to break God's law. Temptation can be broken down into three categories. First, John 2:16 explains how temptation is activated in our lives. *"For all that is in the world, the lust of the flesh, and the lust of the eyes, and the pride of life, is not of the Father, but is of the world."* The lust of the flesh refers to the cravings of sinful man. It describes those sinful things that make us feel good. Eve saw that the fruit was good for food (the lust of the eyes). So many things seem to be beautiful to us, and we must have them right away. It describes our sinful desire for material possessions. The fruit was pleasant to Eve's eyes (the pride of life). Almost everyone is full of his or her own self-importance. It describes the notion that we are better than the next person. Eve saw that the fruit could make her wise and a god.

Temptation is a process from holiness to sinfulness. Few temptations drop us in sin's deep end immediately. Instead, we are led there gradually. James 1:13-15 speaks of this ... *"Let no man say when he is tempted, I am tempted of God: for God cannot be tempted with evil, neither tempteth he any man: But every man is tempted, when he is drawn away of his own lust, and enticed. Then when lust hath conceived, it bringeth forth sin: and sin, when it is finished, bringeth forth death."* (KJV). That is exactly why the devil presents temptation to us. He wants us to fall into sin and to be spiritually doomed. Is it not true that we are usually tempted to meet our own physical needs? These needs, once met, turn into bondage, and bondage brings us to death. Temptation is satan's bait on the hook of sin, and once captivated, he only has to reel us in.

Regardless of how successful a person might consider himself in getting away with his adventure into sin, we could learn a few things from David. First, however, we must note Numbers 32:23, *"But if you fail to keep your word, then you will have sinned against the LORD, and you may be sure that your sin will find you out."* Interestingly, the context of this verse is a warning to those who may not be faithful to their words of promise.

Overall, this story is a quick study into cause and effect. First, it teaches that, regardless of one's status, adultery cannot be committed without damaging relationships any more than murder can be committed without damaging relationships. It does not matter whether the perpetrator is a prince or pauper. The only variable is the speed with which the effect takes place. We should never forget the warning given in Genesis 2:17, *"except the tree of the knowledge of good and evil. If you eat its fruit, you are sure to die."* The wages of sin is death (See Romans 6:23) no matter which commandment is broken.

Besides death, sin produces two effects that may also manifest slowly. First, sin causes a damaged relationship with God. Isaiah 59:1-2 shows that sin creates a division between God and us because of the breach of trust. Sin is a breaking of the terms of the covenant agreed on by both God and us. After committing a sin like adultery, can the individual be trusted any longer? This effect is not easily seen, but God's Word nonetheless reveals it does occur. As this episode shows, with repentance and God's merciful forgiveness, the division can be healed.

Second, sin causes evil results in our lives in this world. Even with God's forgiveness, this second effect remains and must be borne by the sinner—and tragically, by those sinned against. For example, the evil effects of David's sin brought death—either directly or indirectly—to five people. It directly caused the deaths of Uriah and the newborn son of David and Bathsheba. In addition, it greatly intensified the ultimately deadly competition between Absalom, Amnon, and Adonijah, all of whom died violently. With the dishonorable example of their father before their eyes, it could only teach disrespect, even for those closest to them.

Thus, the throne fell to Solomon. He never had to live through the kind of family life that David's older children did. When he committed similar sins, he could never say that he saw his father do the same things. Nevertheless, David's habitual sins transferred down his family tree.

That brings us to the topic of habitual sin. Have you ever heard the statement, "If you're not willing to stop sinning, you shouldn't even call yourself a Christian"? If that were true, then why did God say David was a man after His own heart? I think much of our difficulty in understanding how God could apply this phrase to a man who became an adulterer and murderer comes from the way we use the phrase today. For us, it means "just the kind of guy I like" or "someone who does what I would do in a situation." But that is not what the phrase means when Samuel uses it to describe to Saul, the kind of king God is seeking to establish a dynasty in Israel.

The Hebrew phrase is actually "a man *according to* God's heart"—one who is in accordance with God's wishes for the kingship. Samuel makes this clear by observing, "You have not kept the LORD's command," that is, that the kingship should not be treated as divine or as encompassing priestly powers.

David set an example for all subsequent kings by never acting as if he were a divine king or priest-king. Uzziah, by contrast, one of his successors, was punished for going into the temple of the LORD to burn incense, effectively claiming to be a priest-king. The priests challenged him, saying, "It is not right for you, Uzziah, to burn incense to the LORD. That is for the priests." Uzziah was smitten with leprosy and had to turn over royal power to his son as regent. "His pride led to his downfall," the biblical narrator observes.

David was always devoted to the LORD as Israel's supreme ruler, and he never turned aside after other gods. This heart of loyalty became the standard by which all later kings were judged. The Bible says about Abijah, for example, *"He committed the same sins as his father before him, and he was not faithful to the LORD his God, as his ancestor David had been."* We might think of a "man after God's own heart" as one whose heart is fully devoted to God.

Nevertheless, even such men and women need to be very careful about how they respond to the challenges and especially the disappointments of life. David committed adultery after his army officers, out of a commendable desire to protect his life, made him stay back in Jerusalem when they went out to war. For a military commander like David, this idleness and apparent uselessness were hard to bear. One may surmise that he tried to find renewed validation by getting a beautiful woman for himself,

Bathsheba.

He should have regarded her as strictly off-limits because she was another man's wife—in fact, the wife of one of his trusted "mighty warriors," Uriah the Hittite. Instead, David abused his kingly powers and committed adultery and murder to get her. In a divine judgment, his royal house was torn apart in the next generation. So no divine approval of David's actions can be found in the earlier description of him as a "man after God's own heart."

So, before you agree with this statement, let us analyze a few things. First, Christians do not claim to be sinless—quite the opposite. First, John says, *"If we claim we have no sin, we are only fooling ourselves and not living in the truth."* (1 John 1:8). Second, if you actually talk to a person struggling with a habitual sin, what you are almost certain to find is that they are very willing to stop sinning—they just do not know how to do it. I know a whole lot of people stuck in habitual sin, and, consistently, they hate the thing, they do not want to do the thing, they have tried all kinds of stuff to prevent it, and nothing has worked. Willingness is not the problem.

That brings us to the second statement many religious people make, "The answer to habitual sin is to just stop it." Only someone who has never faced something impossible would say this. Paul, who wrote most of the New Testament—said this, *"For what I do is not the good I want to do; no, the evil I do not want to do—this I keep on doing. ... What a wretched man I am! Who will rescue me from this body of death?"* (Romans 7:19-24). Paul's answer to his struggle was that he needed Jesus Christ to change him, that his willpower was not enough. He wrote about this in the book of Galatians, when he chastised the people there for trying to live the Christian life "by human effort" (See Galatians 3:3).

One of the ways Jesus changes us is to give us wisdom about what is driving us to that sin in the first place. For example, maybe for some people, their sin of habit is pornography—and they feel guilty about it. However, very few of them have ever thought and prayed on the question, "What's driving me to look at this in the first place?" A big motivator for some is that they use pornography as a stress release. Well, now, if we want to move past this habitual sin, we would need to learn how to live a lower-stress life and learn what godly, healthy stress relievers look like. However, we would never come to that point if we had clenched our teeth and decided to "just stop it" in our own strength. So, what is the root issue of your sin of habit?

Another common statement in the church says, "If you're stuck in habitual sin, you should question whether or not you're really saved." Really? Here is what the Bible says, *"For 'everyone who calls on the name of the LORD will be saved.'"* (Romans 10:13). If you have said, "Jesus, I'm a sinner, and I'm asking You to forgive me and take control of my life and heart," you are as saved as saved can be.

These kinds of Christians are confused about how we move past a sin. The truth is that we move forward, one step at a time, with wisdom guiding the journey. Human willpower and "best intentions" do not lead to changed lives.

The main thing that our well-meaning brothers and sisters are confused about, though, is the nature of God's forgiveness. The truth is—it just does not run out. Jesus said if your brother wrongs you the same way seven times in a single day, you should forgive him (See Luke 17:4). That means, you should be prepared to forgive the same person 70 times seven times (See Matthew 18:22). In other words, Jesus is saying, "do not keep a record of wrong." The Bible tells us our forgiveness of others is to mirror God's forgiveness of us (See Ephesians 4:32).

What all this means is that God has an unbelievably high ability to forgive us, which is good, because we have a ridiculously high tendency to sin. Is that not exactly what the Bible says? *"God's law was given so that all people could see how sinful they were. But as people sinned more and more, God's wonderful grace became more abundant."* (Romans 5:20).

If you are struggling with habitual sin, first, welcome to being human and a Christian. We have all been there. Do not panic. God is not going to smack you with a mammoth stick if you do something wrong. Ask God for wisdom. Seek out some older Christians who are mature about the subject. Seek the Lord on what is driving the sin areas in your life. Systematically, address those behind-the-scenes problems, and you will begin to see God change your life right in front of you. Realize that on your own, you have no power over sin in your life. Only Jesus has that power to overcome all that is worldly about you. So just remember, being set free from sin is a process. Some people still struggle with the fact that they continue to sin because they have not understood that salvation is a process. In fact, salvation is a three-stage process.

Is there a conflict inside you between the old sinful nature you were born with and the new nature you were given when you accepted Christ? That is why Galatians

5:17 says, *"The sinful nature wants to do evil, which is just the opposite of what the Spirit wants. And the Spirit gives us desires that are the opposite of what the sinful nature desires. These two forces are constantly fighting each other, so you are not free to carry out your good intentions."* When you try to fight the battle in your own strength, it leads to three results: frustration, confusion, and desperation.

Sometimes you feel like Dr. Jekyll and Mr. Hyde. One minute you are a wonderful Christian person who wants to love the Lord and please God in everything you do. Then there is this old "you" from years ago. The one who thinks he can do everything himself. *"So the trouble is not with the law, for it is spiritual and good. The trouble is with me, for I am all too human, a slave to sin. I don't really understand myself, for I want to do what is right, but I don't do it. Instead, I do what I hate.* (Romans 7:14-15). When you try to overcome sin in your own strength, confusion reigns.

The second reaction we have when we try to follow the law of God in our own strength is that we get frustrated. *"And I know that nothing good lives in me, that is, in my sinful nature. I want to do what is right, but I can't."* (Romans 7:18). Struggling with sin is frustrating. You want to change. No matter how hard you try, you just cannot. You are motivated. Nevertheless, you do not have the determination. You have the desire to do what is right. For some reason, you cannot do it. *"For no one can ever be made right with God by doing what the law commands. The law simply shows us how sinful we are."* (Romans 3:20).

It will not do you any good just to get confused and frustrated over sin. Hopefully confusion and frustration will lead you to desperation. Frankly, you need to get desperate if you want to have a win over sin. Paul came to the place in his life where he just could not take it anymore. He cried out, *"Oh, what a miserable person I am! Who will free me from this life that is dominated by sin and death?"* (Romans 7:24). It all boils down to this: are you willing to stop trying to fix everything yourself?

Confusion, frustration, and desperation with sin lead to an opportunity to change. It is called repentance. True repentance is not worldly sorrow. Paul told the Corinthians, "I perceive that you have worldly sorrow," or some of your translations will say, "worldly grief," and that is because non-Christians can feel bad. When someone who is not a Christian does something wrong, he or she says something like this, "I feel bad. Why is that?" The answer is, you are bad. You feel bad because you are bad. There is no need to dig for some deep psychological investigation. You feel bad because you are bad. God gave you a conscience. We were created in His image. We can grieve, quench, and resist the Holy Spirit, but the Holy Spirit works through our conscience, as Jesus promised He would, to convict us of sin (See John 16:13).

What happens in worldly sorrow, or grief, is we feel bad, but we do not change. Too many do not repent when they are caught. The opposite of repenting is being caught. You have to say, "I am really sorry. I did a horrible thing. I feel really bad." The psalmist says, "Against you only, Lord God, have I sinned." When celebrities are caught in an unbecoming act, they go to Barbara Walters, Larry King, Oprah, or Dr. Phil. We go get somebody to set up their stage for their show, their set, like a confessional. Rehab is our cultural version of repentance. Everybody has to go to rehab. If you have done something bad, you have got to go to rehab: drug rehab, sex rehab, or alcohol rehab. Then we hear statements, like, "My dad didn't hug me." They go to rehab for a while, and you pay their dues.

Real repentance is not blame-shifting, which is, "Yeah, something bad happened, but it's their fault." This goes all the way back to the garden. Adam sinned and said, "God, you made a woman. She is defective. The two of you need to sort this out." Eve says, "Oh, don't look at me; the devil made me do it." The truth is that they both were morally responsible for their own transgression. "Yes, I stole from my boss, but after all, they weren't paying me enough." "I did cheat on my spouse, but they were not meeting my needs." A victim mentality is always blaming someone else.

Real repentance is also not minimizing. What happened was you sinned, someone calls you to repent, and the first thing you do is find someone who has done something worse. "At least I didn't kill someone." You try to find someone worse than you are. "You're a terrible spouse." "Well, at least you're not married to so and so." If all else fails, hit the Hitler button, that is what people do. "At least I'm not a Nazi." Yeah, compared to Hitler, everyone looks good. It is minimizing. "Oh, it's not a big deal. You are freaking out. You are overreacting. Why do you have to get so emotional?"

Additionally, real repentance is not making excuses. "Yeah, I did it, but I had a rough upbringing. You know, I did not get a good education. My dad did not hug me. I am genetically dysfunctional."

True repentance is not religious repentance. Religious repentance is this, "I see your sin, not my own. I confess your sin, not my own. I'm really unhappy with your sin, but I'm not really troubled by my own." It is because religious people tend to think that they are self-righteous, pious, holy, and better than everyone else. The result is that they think they are good, and everyone else is bad. They are always glad to talk about all the things you have done wrong, but they never say things like, "It was my fault. I'm sorry. I was wrong." Religious people are notorious for overlooking their own sin and talking about everyone else's, sometimes couching it in the form of a prayer request so that it looks particularly holy when it is not.

True repentance is also not mere confession. Mere confession is very confusing, particularly for Christians, because it is when someone sins, and you confront, or rebuke them, call them to repentance as John does. You say, "That was really wrong."

Then they say, "You know what? You're right, that was terrible."

You say, "Oh good, I'm glad you recognized that. Let me hug you, and we're all better now."

Then they do it again. You say, "I thought you were sorry."

"Oh, I was. I'm sorry again, and I'll be sorry next week, and the week after that. I'm sorry a lot. And every time I do it, at least I'm not a hypocrite, I'm authentic, I'm honest, I'm real, I'm true." Mere confession is an acknowledgment of sin, without a repentance of sin.

Many understand the term repentance to mean "turning from sin." This is not the biblical definition of repentance. In the Bible, repent means "to change one's mind." The Bible also tells us that true repentance will result in a change of actions (See Luke 3:8-14; Acts 3:19). Acts 26:20

declares, *"I preached first to those in Damascus, then in Jerusalem and throughout all Judea, and also to the Gentiles, that all must repent of their sins and turn to God—and prove they have changed by the good things they do."* The full biblical definition of repentance is a change of mind that results in a change of action.

It is crucially important that we understand repentance is not a work we do to earn salvation. No one can repent and come to God unless God pulls that person to Himself (See John 6:44). Acts 5:31 and 11:18 indicate that repentance is something God gives—it is only possible because of His grace. No one can repent unless God grants repentance. All of salvation, including repentance and faith, is a result of God drawing us, opening our eyes, and changing our hearts. God's longsuffering leads us to repentance (See 2 Peter 3:9), as does His kindness (Romans 2:4). While repentance is not a work that earns salvation, repentance unto salvation does result in works. It is impossible to change your mind truly and fully without that causing a change in action. In the Bible, repentance results in a change in behavior. That is why John the Baptist called people to "produce fruit in keeping with repentance" (See Matthew 3:8). A person who has truly repented from rejection of Christ to faith in Christ will give evidence of a changed life (See 2 Corinthians 5:17; Galatians 5:19-23; James 2:14-26).

A WORD OF THOUGHT

"Repent therefore and be converted, that your sins may be blotted out, so that times of refreshing may come from the presence of the Lord." (Acts 3:19 - KJV)

"All the prophets testify about him that everyone who believes in him receives forgiveness of sins through his name." (Acts 10:43 - NIV)

"Therefore let us leave the elementary teachings about Christ and go on to maturity, not laying again the foundation of repentance from acts that lead to death, and of faith in God, instruction about baptisms, the laying on of hands, the resurrection of the dead, and eternal judgment. And God permitting, we will do so." (Heb. 6:1-3 - NIV)

"For thou, Lord, art good, and ready to forgive; and plenteous in mercy unto all them that call upon thee." (Psalm 86:5 - KJV)

"Come to me, all you who labor and are heavy laden, and I will give you rest. Take My yoke upon you and learn from Me, for I am gentle and lowly in heart, and you will find rest for your souls. For My yoke is easy and My burden is light." (Matthew 11:28-30 - KJV)

"Peter replied, "Repent and be baptized, every one of you, in the name of Jesus Christ for the forgiveness of your sins. And you will receive the gift of the Holy Spirit." (Acts 2:38- NIV)

"In him we have redemption through his blood, the forgiveness of sins, in accordance with the riches of God's grace." (Ephesians 1:7 - NIV)

"Therefore confess your sins to each other and pray for each other so that you may be healed. The prayer of a righteous man is powerful and effective." (James 5:16 - NIV)

"For he has rescued us from the dominion of darkness and brought us into the kingdom of the Son he loves." (Colossians 1:13 - NIV)

"I, even I, am He who blots out your transgressions for My own sake; and I will not remember your sins. Put Me in remembrance; let us contend together; state your case, that you may be acquitted." (Isaiah 43:25-26 - KJV)

"Cast your burden on the Lord, and He shall sustain you; He shall never permit the righteous to be moved." (Psalm 55:2 - KJV)

5

DEAR DOUBLE MINDED MAN

WHEN YOU WERE A CHILD, AND at the playground, were you ever tempted to climb the slide without using the ladder? Most of us have probably gone up the wrong way, but there is something about climbing the slide that way that we find appealing. Unfortunately, some Christians live their life as if they are on a slide. Jesus said, *"You can enter God's Kingdom only through the narrow gate. The highway to hell is broad, and its gate is wide for the many who choose that way. But the gateway to life is very narrow and the road is difficult, and only a few ever find it."* (Matthew 7:13-14).

I am sure we can picture in our minds different ways to visualize what Jesus is saying, but I want to use the slide to illustrate what Jesus is saying. Whether we are climbing the stairs or climbing the slide to get to the top, it is always more tiring and difficult than sliding down because gravity takes over. Here is what Christians do sometimes. When it comes to Sunday, they start climbing the slide and heading in the right direction even though it is more difficult, but as soon as Sunday is over, they throw their hands in the air and slide back down toward the broad road that leads to destruction.

The double-minded man, some Christians more than

others, live a religious life on one hand and worldly life on the other. The problem with living a double life is that eventually, your sin will find you out. Even if you are not caught red-handed, your sinful life will eventual come into your religious life. *"Beware of false prophets who come disguised as harmless sheep but are really vicious wolves. You can identify them by their fruit, that is, by the way they act. Can you pick grapes from thorn bushes, or figs from thistles? A good tree produces good fruit, and a bad tree produces bad fruit. A good tree can't produce bad fruit, and a bad tree can't produce good fruit. So every tree that does not produce good fruit is chopped down and thrown into the fire. Yes, just as you can identify a tree by its fruit, so you can identify people by their actions."* (Matthew 7:15-20)

If you want to see Christians at their best behavior, just come to church. It is easy to look and sound like a Christian at church because the worldly temptations are not on our minds. We have our minds set on being Christians, and those who are striving to live the Christian life surround us. Even those Christians who are living a double life will not bring their sinful lifestyle into the church. It is amazing how people can change their behavior when they are in the house of God. The husband and wife who have been fighting all day can come to church, open the door, put a big smile on their face, sit next to each other, and pretend everything is okay. Another Christian could have been cursing up a storm just before church, and saying all kinds of vile things, but when they enter the church building, their speech changes because they check their filthy mouth at the door.

It does not matter what the sin is, Christians will leave

that sin at the door when they come to church. While they are at church, they do their best to climb up that slide, but the problem is they are just pretending to be Christians. Now I have no doubt that they want to be that person they are pretending to be, and they want to be known as a faithful Christian who lives their lives 24/7 for God, but the truth of the matter is, they are not.

They have serious issues that are eating away at them and causing them to slide down the slide much more than they are trying to climb up on it. Deep down, they know what they are doing is wrong, but the problem is, they have had their conscience seared with a hot iron. *"Now the Holy Spirit tells us clearly that in the last times some will turn away from the true faith; they will follow deceptive spirits and teachings that come from demons. These people are hypocrites and liars, and their consciences are dead."* (1 Timothy 4:1,2).

At first, when a faithful Christian realizes what he is doing is sinful, he will feel guilty about it because his conscience is speaking to him and telling him this is wrong. For most Christians, that is enough to keep them from repeating that sin, but other Christians keep fighting against their conscience until they no longer feel the guilt even though they know what they are doing is wrong. For this reason, their conscience has become seared with a hot iron.

One of the most dangerous places a Christian can find himself is with a seared conscience. Nothing is going to hold you back from your pretend Christian lives, and you will get to the point where you do not even make an effort to climb back up that slide because it is so much easier to slide down that broad road that leads to destruction.

I told you how Christians would leave their sin at the

door when they come to church, but guess what. When they leave the church building, they will pick it right back up on the way out. The husband and wife will continue their fight, that one Christian will curse and say filthy things all the way home. Again, this is about living the double life.

Christians are on their best behavior when their peers surround them. Those Christians who are living the double life would think twice about saying or doing some of the things they normally do if another Christian brother or sister were there with them. While this is not a practical solution, it might help you if you would imagine that if your brethren were there with you. You can ask yourself, would I dare say this or do this thing while they were watching and listening?

Even more than that, we must remind ourselves that God is there, and He knows what we are doing. We cannot hide anything from Him. Imagine yourself saying or doing that sinful thing with Jesus watching you. Would you do it? Do you think Jesus would approve? If not, do not do it. It never ceases to amaze me how easy it is for us to forget about God and how we seem willing to face His wrath for our disobedience. We start thinking God will forgive us anyway, so we might as well indulge in some worldly sins.

We need to remember what the writer of Hebrews says: *"Dear friends, if we deliberately continue sinning after we have received knowledge of the truth, there is no longer any sacrifice that will cover these sins. There is only the terrible expectation of God's judgment and the raging fire that will consume his enemies. For anyone who refused to obey the law of Moses was put to death without mercy on the testimony of two or three witnesses. . Just think how much worse the punishment will be for those who have trampled on the Son of God, and have treated the blood of the covenant, which made us holy, as if it were common and unholy, and have insulted and disdained the Holy Spirit who brings God's mercy to us."* (Hebrews 10:26-29).

As many reality shows that have been made over the years, I am sure most of us have seen a show where they constantly record what is going on in a house or some kind of game environment. At first, some people will be on their best behavior because they know the world is watching them, but given enough time, most of them become comfortable with the cameras, and their true colors begin to rear their ugly head on national TV.

Well, this same thing happens with Christians who are living the double life. Even though they know that God is watching them, they get comfortable with that, they completely ignore it, and they let their true colors rear their ugly head. They will lie to their spouse, their friends, or to whomever they can because they find joy in lying even though they know it is a sin.

Some Christians lose their Christianity altogether when they get around their worldly friends. They will cuss like them, tell filthy jokes, and even get drunk on alcohol with them even though they know that it is wrong, and they know that God is watching.

Other Christians have the attitude that if they are by themselves and no one is around that if they start viewing pornography on the internet that they are not harming anyone, and so they indulge in the sin of the lust of the flesh, even though God is watching and knows exactly what they are doing. I think the internet makes some Christians ignorant because they seem to think the internet is some other world that God cannot see or is a safe zone where a Christian can act however they want to. There is a big generation gap in this church when it comes to using computers and the internet. Therefore, what I am about to tell you is not going to apply to some of you because some of you do not know much about computers or the internet.

Nevertheless, I want to make you aware of how some are using it so you can at least be aware of what your children and grandchildren are being exposed to and why I said that the internet makes some Christians ignorant.

On the internet, two of the most popular social networks are Facebook and Twitter. For the most part, these social networks are designed for teenagers, but many adults use them as well. One benefit of social networks is that you can easily find your old high school friends and send them a note. You can upload pictures, videos and give information about yourself and what you are doing. If you have a website, you can let people know about it so they can visit. On the other hand, some Christians seem to think that these social networks are nothing but fun and games, and they view it as a fantasy world in which it does not matter what they say or do. Some Christians will get on these networks and show their true colors. They will type vulgar and rude messages that everyone can see that is on their friend's list. They will use services like YouTube or something similar to record videos or audio of themselves saying and doing all kinds of sinful things. They do all this without thinking about what kind of example they are being or how they influence others to be sinful.

This is the reason I say that the internet makes some Christians ignorant. There is nothing wrong with using the services the right way, and there is nothing wrong with

Christians talking about things such as sports, politics, or other matters they are passionate about. However, a Christian should keep their language clean and not sound like the world when they do so, but more and more Christians leave their Christianity at the door when it comes to the internet.

Another technology that works with the internet and social networks is cell phones. The cell phone is a great convenience, but some have made it to something evil. If you go to any public place that has changing rooms, you might see a sign that says, no cells phones allowed. Some have no idea why, but I am going to tell you why. Most cell phones have cameras built-in, and girls will go into the bathroom, take pictures of other girls while they are showering or changing, and then take those photos and either send them to their friend via their cell phone, or they will post them on the internet, including on these social networks. This happens with people as well, but it happens to girls more.

I wish I could tell you that Christians were not involved in such practices, but the truth of the matter is, some have been because they view it as a game and not reality.

Some Christians will take their own picture in various ways and post them, thinking that only a few will see it. But, Christians need to understand that once they place an image of themselves on the internet, it is almost impossible to get it off because even if you remove it, you do not know who copied and put it somewhere else, and then you are going be stuck with that image being on the net for years.

Almost 2000 years ago today, Peter said, *"Stay alert! Watch out for your great enemy, the devil. He prowls around like a roaring lion, looking for someone to devour. Stand firm against him, and be strong in your faith. Remember that your Christian brothers and sisters all over the world are going through the same kind of suffering you are."* (1 Peter 5:8-9).

The devil will never cease to try and bring you down. He will use whatever worldly devices he can to make you live a double life. He loves for you to think that the things you do on the internet or in private do not really matter. He has his iron ready and he is willing to help you sear your conscience.

I do not know about you, but this makes me angry at sin. I cannot stand to see how my fellow Christians are being drugged down the slide to the broad road of destruction. It makes me angry how sin is ensnaring our people and causing them to act just like the world. We have to break this ugly cycle of living a double life because God wants us to live for Him. He wants us to honor the commitment we made to stand against the evil way.

Even if your conscience has been seared with a hot iron, it is not too late for you because God has the power to help break you free from the shackles of sin, but you must be willing to make an effort. You must be willing to stop living the double life and thinking it is okay to act like the world, and abuse alcohol and drugs like them. We have to engrain in our heads that living like the world is not worth it as Jesus said, *"And what do you benefit if you gain the whole world but lose your own soul? Is anything worth more than your soul?"* (Matthew 16:26).

We need to recommit ourselves to God. We need to be like Josiah because when Moses Law was found and was read to him: *"When the king heard what was written in the*

Law, he tore his clothes in despair." (2 Chronicles 34:19). Josiah was devastated by what he heard from the Law of Moses because he realized that his people had not been following God. He learned that God would punish his people, but since Josiah had such a sincere heart in restoring his life and the life of his people back to following God, God put off the punishment until a later time. Josiah got busy right away.

Then the king summoned all the elders of Judah and Jerusalem. And the king went up to the Temple of the LORD with all the people of Judah and Jerusalem, along with the priests and the Levites—all the people from the greatest to the least. There the king read to them the entire Book of the Covenant that had been found in the LORD's Temple. The king took his place of authority beside the pillar and renewed the covenant in the LORD's presence. He pledged to obey the LORD by keeping all his commands, laws, and decrees with all his heart and soul. He promised to obey all the terms of the covenant that were written in the scroll. And he required everyone in Jerusalem and the people of Benjamin to make a similar pledge. The people of Jerusalem did so, renewing their covenant with God, the God of their ancestors.

So Josiah removed all detestable idols from the entire land of Israel and required everyone to worship the LORD their God. And throughout the rest of his lifetime, they did not turn away from the LORD, the God of their ancestors. (2 Chronicles 34:29-33)

This is what we must do as Christians. We must examine ourselves and, if we see that our actions do not match up with God's Word, then we must renew our commitment to God and start taking a stand for righteousness. We must change our ways to His ways. We must remove the abominations from our lives so we can stop living the double life and start living for Christ.

A WORD OF THOUGHT

"I hate the double-minded, but I love your law." (Psalm 119:113 - NKJV)

"Therefore submit to God. Resist the devil and he will flee from you. Draw near to God and He will draw near to you. Cleanse your hands, you sinners; and purify your hearts, you double-minded." (James 4:7-8 - NKJV)

"Once you were dead because of your disobedience and your many sins. You used to live in sin, just like the rest of the world, obeying the devil—the commander of the powers in the unseen world. He is the spirit at work in the hearts of those who refuse to obey God." (Ephesians 2:1-2)

"For let not that man suppose that he will receive anything from the Lord; he is a double-minded man, unstable in all his ways." (James 1:7-8 - NKJV)

"Don't copy the behavior and customs of this world, but let God transform you into a new person by changing the way you think. Then you will learn to know God's will for you, which is good and pleasing and perfect." (Romans 12:2)

6

DEAR BACKSLIDER, COME HOME

BACKSLIDING HAS BECOME A VERY common feature in all churches now. Many professing Christians believe that they are saved forever simply because of something they did years ago. However, being a Christian means continually living like God wants you to live. Sadly, some believers have "backslidden" into their former sinful way of living. Backsliding is a term signifying what happens when a Christian, who is devoted to God, begins to take his or her relationship with Him less seriously. There are different reasons a believer would backslide, and we will discuss it further in this chapter. The terrible reality is that, if a believer does not stop backsliding, they could wind up without any faith at all.

When we hear the word backslide, it generally conjures up images of falling into open, even gross, sin. While backsliding certainly includes that, it is not necessarily limited to it.

Backsliding is not just falling backward, but it is also failing to go forward spiritually. If we are not moving forward in Christ, then we are naturally going backward. In the Christian life, there is no standing still. We are either progressing or regressing. You show me a person who is failing to move forward spiritually, and by that I mean a person who is not growing as a follower of Jesus, who is not deepening in his or her prayer life and study of Scripture and likeness to Jesus, and I will show you a person who has begun the process of backsliding.

Backsliding is a uniquely biblical word. In Jeremiah 2:19, God says, *"Your wickedness will bring its own punishment. Your turning from me will shame you. You will see what an evil, bitter thing it is to abandon the LORD your God and not fear him."* Also, Jeremiah 3:22 says, *"Return, you backsliding children, and I will heal your backslidings."* (KJV).

The Bible tells the story of a man who backslid, someone whom no one probably expected to fall away. It is the story of Simon Peter and his denial of Jesus Christ. Peter had walked with the Lord during three years of intensive discipleship, and yet Peter denied Him. It is a reminder to us that any of us have the potential to fall.

Peter's denial was not merely a spontaneous response to unexpected danger or embarrassment. For all practical purposes, he had already laid out the groundwork for desertion. No one suddenly backslides. A series of steps always lead to it because we are either building up or weakening our spiritual character every day. We are either moving forward or falling backward.

What led to Peter's fall? Luke 22:33 tells us that Peter said to Jesus, *"Lord, I am ready to go with You, both to prison and to death."* (NKJV). Peter was boasting in the wrong thing; his own strength. Mark's gospel tells us he did this repeatedly. He was prideful and self-assured. The Bible warns, *"Let him who thinks he stands take heed lest he fall"* (1 Corinthians 10:12 - KJV). We should not be confident in ourselves, but in God.

Peter's failure to pray that night in the garden was a direct result of his first sin—the sin of self-confidence. When the disciples accompanied Jesus to the Mount of Olives, He specifically instructed Peter, James, and John to pray (See Luke 22:40). However, they fell asleep. They failed in praying. If they were not so full of self-confidence, I am sure they would have been praying.

Too often, we do the same. We do not pray. We take matters into our own hands, come up with clever little plans, and make a big mess out of things. We need to call upon the Lord. We need to recognize our own weakness. This brings us to Peter's next step down.

In Luke 22:54, we read, *"And Peter followed at a distance."* Distance from the Lord in closeness and fellowship will always be at the foundation of all spiritual regression. In his defense, Peter was still following, but at a distance. It was a half-hearted commitment.

To Peter's credit, he got together with the other disciples after Jesus' crucifixion. Peter had fallen. He was devastated. He was destroyed. However, he was waiting there with the other disciples when Jesus appeared.

Just like Peter, you have a choice when you fail. You can be destroyed and devastated and let the devil pile on the condemnation, and you can be history. Or, you can get back to Jesus as quickly as possible.

We must realize that if Peter, a disciple of our Lord, could backslide, the possibility remains with us. The reality of the danger of backsliding is made clear by the many admonitions in Scripture warning of this possibility. There would be no need to warn anyone of something that could never happen. As he instructs his student Timothy, the apostle Paul writes, *"Timothy, my son, here are my instructions for you, based on the prophetic words spoken about you earlier. May they help you fight well in the Lord's battles. Cling to your faith in Christ, and keep your conscience clear. For some people have deliberately violated their consciences; as a result, their faith has been shipwrecked."* (1 Timothy 1:18-19). Paul encourages Timothy, and those to whom he ministers, to make sure they are diligent in nurturing their faith. To neglect this is to open the real possibility of ruining their faith, as he writes that some have already done.

A warning found in Hebrews seems even more pointed, *"Be careful then, dear brothers and sisters. Make sure that your own hearts are not evil and unbelieving, turning you away from the living God. You must warn each other every day, while it is still "today," so that none of you will be deceived by sin and hardened against God."* (Hebrews 3:12-13). Speaking to professing believers, the writer of Hebrews admonishes them to search their hearts for signs of 'evil' or 'unbelief.' That the writer considers his audience to be believers is shown in that he addresses them as "brothers." This is a clear warning that it is possible to fall away from God if one is not careful to keep one's faith alive and active.

Jesus tells the parable of the soils in Mark 4:14-19. This parable describes the heart of the person who hears the Word of God. While this parable directly speaks of the person who is first hearing the Word of God, it indirectly describes the hearts of any hearer of the Word. *"The farmer plants seed by taking God's word to others. The seed that fell on the footpath represents those who hear the message, only to have Satan come at once and take it away."* (Mark 4:14-15).

This type of person, who hears the Word of God, knows what he or she should do but does nothing or is a procrastinator. While possibly taking the initial step towards faith, but no subsequent steps are taken, and no commitment is made—it is a missed opportunity. Sadly, if one does not act while the Holy Spirit is prompting, the opportunity may not come again.

"The seed on the rocky soil represents those who hear the message and immediately receive it with joy. But since they don't have deep roots, they don't last long. They fall away as soon as they have problems or are persecuted for believing God's word." (Mark 4:16-17). These people enthusiastically embrace their newfound faith but never do anything to solidify it or to make sure they are growing. They consider the one-time act of praying a prayer or signing a card to be all that is necessary for living the Christ-like life. Soon, the newness wears off; they have no true foundation, and, before they realize it, they have returned to their old way of life.

"And others are the ones sown among thorns. They are those who hear the word, but the cares of the world and the deceitfulness of riches and the desires for other things enter in and choke the word, and it proves unfruitful." (Mark 4:18-19). These people take their eyes off Jesus. They fail to trust in Him to see them through the hard times. They allow their selfish desires to overrule their allegiance to God. It might be that the love of money (I Timothy 6:10) outweighs their love of God. It might be that they simply do not trust that God will provide as He promises. These believers allow the things of the world (See James 4:4) to turn them away from God.

However, there are those who hear God's Word and

receive it with gladness. Mark 4:20 says, *"And the seed that fell on good soil represents those who hear and accept God's word and produce a harvest of thirty, sixty, or even a hundred times as much as had been planted!"* These people understand that a relationship with God is not simply an add-on to our current sinful lives. It is not simply 'stay-out-of-hell' insurance. A saving relationship with God involves a commitment on our part to live for Him. It requires a radical restructuring of our lives around the will of God. This type of person immerses himself or herself into a relationship with God as being the center of his or her life. This person grows deeper in that relationship every day by praying, studying the Bible, and doing whatever God lays on their heart to do.

Jesus spoke about four types of backsliders in the three parables in Luke 15 represented by the lost sheep, the lost coin, the lost younger son, and the lost elder son.

The lost sheep is a picture of a born-again believer who backslid. He went astray because he lacked fellowship. Perhaps he was alone in a place where there was no good church. Not having a strong enough relationship with the Lord, he was dragged down by his surroundings. Or perhaps, he did not value fellowship with other believers sufficiently and thus went astray. If he had stayed in the midst of the church, he would have been safe. However, perhaps he was self-confident and thus went astray.

There may have been other reasons too why he backslid. The attractions of the world may have proved to be too much for him. Or perhaps he was discouraged by the pressure of trial. He may have been deceived by the craftiness of men and demons. Or he may have been careless in his walk with the Lord and gradually fell away.

The Lord describes His flock in this parable as consisting of "righteous persons WHO NEED NO REPENTANCE" (See Luke 15:7, emphasis added). They do not need any repentance because they are judging themselves all the time and striving to have a conscience without offense towards God and men. They are quick to confess the slightest sinful thought and attitude to God and equally quick to confess the slightest sinful word and deed to men. As a result, they live each day as those who need no repentance—because they repent constantly. The lost sheep did not have this attitude—and so it backslid.

The lost coin was lost due to very different reasons. It was lost because of the failure of the woman. The woman is a picture of a church. She was careless in taking care of her coins. The coin was a silver coin, and silver was used to redeem the firstborn children of Israel in the Old Testament (See Numbers 18:16). So the silver coin speaks of a redeemed child of God (once saved) who is now lost. However, this believer backslid primarily due to the failure of his church. His church was perhaps a dead church where the standards of God's Word were not preached and so they did not care for his eternal soul.

Cain asked the Lord if he was his brother's keeper. He was. In the church, every one of us has a responsibility to keep our brothers and sisters from falling. So this parable is directed not at the backslider as much as at the other members of his church (the woman) who are careless enough to allow a coin to be lost.

The younger son represents yet another type of backslider. He was one who was impatient to launch out on his own—before God's time. He sought his own, loved money, rebelled against his father, and finally left his home.

Here is a believer who wants to receive everything he can, from God and from his elder brothers. However, after he has received everything, he leaves them. Many preachers make use of their connection with their spiritual fathers and thereby get a ministry and a name for themselves. Once they have that, they seek to become independent.

This son is a picture of a believer who does not want the discipline of being subject to God-appointed authority (his father). God's purpose in all discipline is to break His children so that He can commit spiritual authority to them one day. But many, like this younger son, frustrate God's purposes for them and end up with "the pigs!" Only then do some of them come to their senses and return to the Father's house in brokenness and repentance.

The elder son is a picture of a believer who does not look like a backslider. He is a proud, self-righteous believer who compares himself with others and who feels that he has lived a better life and produced better results in his ministry than others.

Instead of humbly acknowledging these blessings as the undeserved mercy of God, he becomes proud of what he thinks he has accomplished. Therefore, God resists him, and very soon, satan is able to knock him down.

The first three backsliders in these parables finally came home. However, in the case of the elder son, we see him outside the house at the end of the story. So, the Lord must have wanted to point him out as the worst backslider of the lot.

The Good Shepherd went after the lost sheep until He found it. We who are under shepherds must have the same attitude. We must go after those who have backslidden from the church through carelessness, satanic deception, and their lusts. It must be the longing of all of us to be *"shepherds after God's own heart"* (See Jeremiah 3:15), who can seek out the many such lost sheep around us today.

Many are quick to criticize these lost sheep, saying that they should not have wandered off on their own, or listened to the voices of false shepherds, etc. However, God is looking for shepherds after His own heart who will go after these lost sheep and bring them back to the fold.

The woman who lost her silver coin was eager to find it. So she did two things. She lit a lamp and swept her house diligently until she found it. These are the two things every church needs to do. First of all, she needs to light a lamp. The life of Jesus is the only true light (See John 1:4), and this is what the church needs to hold up and emphasize at all times. Secondly, there is a lot of rubbish—sin and human traditions in the church—that needs to be swept out completely. Only then will many lost coins be found.

The father of the prodigal son did not go looking for his son when he was lost. He allowed his son to reap the consequences of his rebellion. And when his son came to an end of himself, he came home on his own. He was not carried home on anyone's shoulder, like the lost sheep. He came back when he was totally sick and tired of himself. God's love for such backsliders is shown in His not going after them but allowing them to reap what they have sown.

Many believers, however, lack this wisdom and seek to

carry these rebellious sons on their shoulders into the church. Consequently, they ruin them. On the other hand, these believers do not do much for the lost sheep. Thus because they lack discernment, they console those who should be rebuked and rebuke those who should be consoled.

Feeding rebellious sons of God will only ensure that they never return to God. Such acts are not acts of compassion but acts of folly. Such foolish actions make these lost sons stay out in the far country even longer, and in some cases, forever.

When the prodigal son returned, the father made him sit at his right hand. He did not place his son on probation or make him live in the servant's quarters because his son had come back in brokenness and repentance on his own, without anyone having to persuade him.

When rebellious sons return to the church in true brokenness and repentance, our hearts must be wide open to welcome them. Here is where we see the difference in attitude between those who are like God and those who are like the Pharisees. It will certainly take time for confidence to be restored in such a prodigal son who was once rebellious. However, if he has repented, he must be accepted immediately, warmly, and wholeheartedly, even if he has not been given any ministry in the church for many years.

In the case of the elder son, the father went outside the house and pleaded with him repeatedly. However, the older boy would not yield. Jesus left the story open-ended at this point, leaving it to our imagination to decide what happened to him finally.

There are two possibilities: either, he may have yielded

to his father's pleadings and finally come back home with his head held high. Or he may have rejected his father's pleadings and gone out into the darkness. Whichever way he may have chosen, he lost the place of honor in his home, for that had already been given to his younger brother. The father had already given his ring and the seat at his right hand to his younger son.

There is a vast difference between "prodigal sons" and "elder brothers." Prodigal sons are convinced of their sin on their own, repent deeply, and seek no place of honor in the church. They only want to be slaves until the end of their lives. They are truly broken. "Elder sons," however, have to be repeatedly spoken to before they are convinced. And even when they are convinced, they seek to come back to their place of honor in the church - as kings and not as slaves.

King Saul knew that he had sinned, but he wanted to confess his sin privately to Samuel. He told Samuel, *"I have sinned; but please honour me now before the elders of my people and before Israel"* (1 Samuel 15:30). King David also sinned - far more seriously than Saul, but he wrote a Psalm and acknowledged his sin publicly (See Psalm 51).

Jesus told the Pharisees that their greatest sin was that they sought to justify themselves before men (See Luke 16:15). God hates this sin more than any other. There is very little hope for a backslider who wants to justify himself before men.

God's Word to sinners has always been, *"Only acknowledge your sin"* (See Jeremiah 3:13). Backsliding is not a good idea. God forgives. He will even forgive people for murder, but you might find that the judicial system is not as forgiving. There are consequences for our actions. And the consequences of backsliding are not worth any perceived benefit you might think you will gain in backsliding; (whether it is intentional or just a case of growing cold and drifting away).

One of the consequences of backsliding is wasted time. You are only given so many years on this planet. Your time here is an opportunity to store up treasure in heaven. Another consequence is a loss of credibility. Your friends and family will find it harder to take you very seriously. In addition, your heart becomes harder and indifferent. So if you are even thinking about backsliding then please do not. However, if you have been backslidden, discouraged, and feel that God does not want you back, I want to encourage you because there is hope. He still maintains His position and desire to be your Father.

"For it is impossible to bring back to repentance those who were once enlightened—those who have experienced the good things of heaven and shared in the Holy Spirit, who have tasted the goodness of the word of God and the power of the age to come—and who then turn away from God. It is impossible to bring such people back to repentance; by rejecting the Son of God, they themselves are nailing him to the cross once again and holding him up to public shame." (Hebrews 6:4-6).

If you have gone through a time where you drifted away from the Lord or battled with a sin that just will not go away (like I and many others have), then Hebrews 6:4-6 may be a verse that makes you feel very uncomfortable. It is one of those verses that test our resolve. Are we going to throw in the towel, or are we going to ask (to paraphrase Peter) "where else can we go to find life?" (See John 6:68).

Now if you are searching the internet because you want to find some confidence that God can forgive you, then you are playing Russian roulette. There are good articles and well-meaning articles out there, but they aim to prevent people from backsliding instead of encouraging backsliders to come back to God. Some articles will dissect the meaning of each Greek word and go into a lengthy discussion about Calvinism and Arminianism.

But all you want is confidence, right? You can have great confidence about God's love for you and His willingness to forgive you. To have that confidence, we need to hear what God is saying to us through His entire Word. So how do the experts tell us to examine a verse? Well, one way they might suggest is to use "Hermeneutics." Hermeneutics – it is just an official way of saying "interpret." To interpret a passage of Scripture accurately, we must analyze the context, the wording, and use of the words within Scriptures.

Thankfully, Jesus is our best example of how to interpret Scripture. He looked beyond the literal interpretation to the heart of the message. He summed up the entire law in two commandments: love God with all that you are and love others as you love yourself. That suggests to me that love might just be a key in interpreting Scripture after we have examined the passage. Another example is Jesus healing on the Sabbath. In that case, the law of love and mercy overruled the technical law that effectively said, "Don't do any work on the Sabbath." Yet Jesus is the classic example of the fulfillment of the Sabbath in both practice and spiritual reality. Jesus was always finding time to be alone with God to pray and recharge. (See Luke 9:18).

What does the Bible actually tell us about how God feels about someone who is away from Him? Well, there are difficult passages (Hebrews 6:4-6 is just one example), but there is very good reason to be confident that God loves us and wants to restore us to right relationship with Him. God does not want anyone to be lost (See 2 Peter 3:9). God loves you with an everlasting love (See Jeremiah 31:3). (God was talking to Israel here, but it applies to all believers).

Then there is the prodigal son. How much plainer could Jesus have made it? The lost son walked away from his father, wasted all his money, yet the father welcomed him home as a son, and threw a party to celebrate his return. If that is not enough, then think about what Jesus said in verse 10, "In the same way, there is joy in the presence of God's angels when even one sinner repents." If you are able to make the choice to come back to God, then you can be sure he will welcome you.

"For it is impossible for those who were once enlightened, and have tasted of the heavenly gift, and were made partakers of the Holy Ghost, and have tasted the good word of God, and the powers of the world to come, if they shall fall away, to renew them again unto repentance; SEEING they crucify to themselves the Son of God afresh, and put him to an open shame." (KJV, emphasis added). After reading Hebrews 6:4-6 you probably will have similar questions as I did. The keyword in these verses is the word "seeing." It is a Greek present participle. In other words, "seeing" is a word that expresses a present state of the person who has not changed or repented from walking away from the faith. Let us paraphrase the verse to make more sense: *"Even though you have been a powerful*

Christian at one time, it is impossible for a person who has fallen away to go to heaven, if they remain in the present state of sin . . . they must repent, return to Christ and not expect their past walk with God to carry them, if they are currently rejecting the gospel."

Let us also examine the context. *"Dear friends, even though we are talking this way, we really don't believe it applies to you. We are confident that you are meant for better things, things that come with salvation. For God is not unjust. He will not forget how hard you have worked for him and how you have shown your love to him by caring for other believers, as you still do."* (Hebrews 6:9-10).

The writer of Hebrews is confident that the people reading the letter are not among those who cannot be lead to repentance. How so? Because God is just, and He knows those who are willing to serve Him. One obvious other reason that the writer would have confidence that it does not apply to the reader and that is that someone reading the letter would already have been led to repentance. If you were so cold and indifferent to the things of God that you had completely turned your back on Him, then why would you be reading Hebrews?

We can have great confidence if we flee to God for refuge because He has made promises to us, and it is impossible for God to lie. *"So God has given both his promise and his oath. These two things are unchangeable because it is impossible for God to lie. Therefore, we who have fled to him for refuge can have great confidence as we hold to the hope that lies before us. This hope is a strong and trustworthy anchor for our souls. It leads us through the curtain into God's inner sanctuary. Jesus has already gone in there for us. He has become our eternal High Priest in the order of Melchizedek."* (Hebrews 6:18-20).

So what is the heart of Hebrews chapter six? Flee to God, avoid sin, stay as close as you can to Him, move on to maturity, and confidently cling to the hope that you have through Christ.

God loves you. He is not willing for you to be lost, and whatever Hebrew 6:4-6 might mean literally, it does not contradict Revelation 22:17, *"The Spirit and the bride say, "Come." Let anyone who hears this say, 'Come.' Let anyone who is thirsty come. Let anyone who desires drink freely from the water of life."*

Another thing to take note of is that the word "backslider" or "backsliding" does not appear in the New Testament and is used in the Old Testament primarily of Israel. The Jews, though they were God's chosen people, continually turned their backs on Him and rebelled against His Word (See Jeremiah 8:9). That is why they were forced to make sacrifices for sin repeatedly in order to restore their relationship with the God they had offended. The Christian, however, has availed himself of the perfect, once-and-for-all sacrifice of Christ and needs no further sacrifice for his sin. God himself has obtained our salvation for us (See 2 Corinthians 5:21), and because He saves us, a true Christian cannot fall away so as not to return. This is not eternal security, but security for eternity. God does not walk away from you as some would like to convince you to believe.

Do not misunderstand me; Christians do sin (See 1 John 1:8), but the Christian life is not to be identified by a life of sin. Believers are a new creation (See 2 Corinthians 5:17). We have the Holy Spirit in us producing good fruit

(See Galatians 5:22-23). A Christian life should be a changed life. Christians are forgiven no matter how many times they sin, but at the same time, Christians should live a progressively more holy life as they grow closer to Christ. We should have serious doubts about a person who claims to be a believer yet lives a life that says otherwise. Yes, a true Christian who falls back into sin is still saved, but at the same time, a person who lives a life controlled by sin is not truly a Christian.

What about a person who denies Christ? The Bible tells us that if a person denies Christ, he never truly knew Christ to begin with. First John 2:19 declares, *"These people left our churches, but they never really belonged with us; otherwise they would have stayed with us. When they left, it proved that they did not belong with us."* A person who rejects Christ and turns his back on faith is demonstrating that he never belonged to Christ. Those who belong to Christ remain with Christ. Those who renounce their faith never had it to begin with. Second Timothy 2:11-13 says, *"Here is a trustworthy saying: If we died with him, we will also live with him; if we endure, we will also reign with him. If we disown him, he will also disown us; if we are faithless, he will remain faithful, for he cannot disown himself."*

Again, the concept of a backsliding Christian has long existed within the church, yet does not appear in the New Testament. Instead, the closest biblical reference to a "backslider" is found in the Old Testament account of Jeremiah 8:9. *"These wise teachers will fall into the trap of their own foolishness, for they have rejected the word of the LORD. Are they so wise after all?"* In this account, the Israelites had turned their backs on God. The Lord promised judgment upon them as a result. They would later be removed from the land and deported to Babylon as slaves.

However, in the New Testament, the emphasis is on believing in Jesus as Lord and then living for Him (See John 3:16; Ephesians 2:8-9). Believers are no longer condemned (See Romans 8:1), and nothing can separate a believer from the love of Christ (See Romans 8:38-39).

The New Testament directly answers the issue of a genuine believer who sins. First John 1:8-9 teaches, *"If we say we have no sin, we deceive ourselves, and the truth is not in us. If we confess our sins, he is faithful and just to forgive us our sins and to cleanse us from all unrighteousness."* First, we admit that even as believers, we often sin. Second, we confess our sins and experience forgiveness and cleansing.

In some cases, however, a person can claim to be a Christian for some time but later abandons the faith and claims to deny Jesus Christ. In this case, First John 2:19 offers the proper response: *"These people left our churches, but they never really belonged with us; otherwise they would have stayed with us. When they left, it proved that they did not belong with us."* In other words, a person who claims to be a Christian and later leaves the faith shows he or she was never a genuine believer.

In fact, the apostle Paul taught the church at Corinth to examine themselves to make certain they had believed: *"Examine yourselves to see if your faith is genuine. Test yourselves. Surely you know that Jesus Christ is among you; if not, you have failed the test of genuine faith."* (2 Corinthians 13:5). He did not assume every person in the church was a true believer. Instead, Paul taught the

Corinthians to make certain they had truly believed. His focus was not on whether a person had lost his or her salvation, but whether a person had truly believed at all.

This is the New Testament emphasis in dealing with sinning Christians. The responses are to examine oneself to make certain they are a believer to repent and turn from sin. Believers are to put off the old self and replace this life with the new self. *"Don't lie to each other, for you have stripped off your old sinful nature and all its wicked deeds. Put on your new nature, and be renewed as you learn to know your Creator and become like him."* (Colossians 3:9-10).

A WORD OF THOUGHT

"O LORD, though our iniquities testify against us, do thou it for thy name's sake: for our backslidings are many; we have sinned against thee." (Jeremiah 14:7 - KJV)

"Go and proclaim these words toward the north, and say, Return, thou backsliding Israel, saith the LORD; and I will not cause mine anger to fall upon you: for I am merciful, saith the LORD, and I will not keep anger for ever." (Jeremiah 3:12 - KJV)

"Why then is this people of Jerusalem slidden back by a perpetual backsliding? they hold fast deceit, they refuse to return." (Jeremiah 8:5 - KJV)

"Return, ye backsliding children, and I will heal your backslidings. Behold, we come unto thee; for thou art the LORD our God." (Jeremiah - 3:22)

"How long wilt thou go about, O thou backsliding daughter? for the LORD hath created a new thing in the earth, A woman shall compass a man." (Jeremiah 31:22 - KJV)

"And I saw, when for all the causes whereby backsliding Israel committed adultery I had put her away, and given her a bill of divorce; yet her treacherous sister Judah feared not, but went and played the harlot also." (Jeremiah 3:8)

"The backslider in heart shall be filled with his own ways: and a good man shall be satisfied from himself." (Proverbs 14:14 - KJV)

"Turn, O backsliding children, saith the LORD; for I am married unto you: and I will take you one of a city, and two of a family, and I will bring you to Zion." (Jeremiah 3:14 - KJV)

"But he giveth more grace. Wherefore he saith, God resisteth the proud, but giveth grace unto the humble." (James 4:6 - KJV)

"Let them alone: they be blind leaders of the blind. And if the blind lead the blind, both shall fall into the ditch." (Matthew 15:14 - KJV)

"And he shall turn the heart of the fathers to the children, and the heart of the children to their fathers, lest I come and smite the earth with a curse." (Malachi 4:6 - KJV)

"For Israel slideth back as a backsliding heifer: now the LORD will feed them as a lamb in a large place." (Hosea 4:16 - KJV)

7

DEAR CONFUSED MIND

THERE ARE SOME WHO WANT TO serve God but not sure they can pay the price. For example, the single mother whose only source of income is her abusive boyfriend. The separated mother of four in need of a second income and finds it being with a married man. A young adult whose entire college tuition was paid for by her common law husband. The drug addict who is not sure they can live without the drugs. The con-man who knows no other way of earning an income and the woman who has been a prostitute all her life.

"The LORD was with Jehoshaphat because he followed the example of his father's early years and did not worship the images of Baal. He sought his father's God and obeyed his commands instead of following the evil practices of the kingdom of Israel. He was deeply committed to the ways of the LORD. . . He removed the pagan shrines and Asherah poles from Judah." (2 Chronicles 17:3-4,6). Without a doubt, Jehoshaphat was a godly man. He sought the Lord and walked in His commandments. He took great pride in the ways of the Lord and removed idols from the land. He sent out teachers to instruct the people in God's law (See 2 Chronicles 17:7-9). When a prophet rebuked him for his wrongful alliance with Ahab, unlike his father (See 2

Chronicles 16:10), Jehoshaphat accepted it and went on to institute further religious reforms (See 2 Chronicles 19:2-11).

In chapter 20, we see his heart as a vast army threatens the nation, and he calls the people to prayer and fasting. Jehoshaphat's prayer before the assembly (See 2 Chronicles 20:6-12) reveals his humble trust in the Lord.

The point is, Jehoshaphat was not your average, run-of-the-mill believer. He was a man of strong faith and open godliness who courageously brought reform to the nation. And if *he* suffered from the danger of compromising with the world, then none of us is exempt.

In pointing out Jehoshaphat's problem with wrongful contact with the world, the Bible does not condemn everything the man did, but rather it portrays his strengths and his weaknesses (See 2 Chronicles 19:2-3).

Why did Jehoshaphat, and why do we, fall into the problem of compromise with the world? The first thing we read of Jehoshaphat (See 2 Chronicles 17:1-2) is how he strengthened his position over Israel (Ahab's northern kingdom). Later we read of his valiant army and fortified cities (See 2 Chronicles 17:12-19). He was ready for any onslaught. If Ahab had declared war, Jehoshaphat would have creamed him! Instead, Ahab finagled to get his daughter married to Jehoshaphat's son. The next thing we hear is Jehoshaphat promising the godless Ahab, *"'Will you go with me to Ramoth-gilead?' King Ahab of Israel asked King Jehoshaphat of Judah. Jehoshaphat replied, 'Why, of course! You and I are as one, and my troops are your troops. We will certainly join you in battle.'"* (2 Chronicles 18:3). Unbelievable! It is as if a wrestler had trained for the big event, and his opponent invited him out for dinner and slipped poison into his coffee.

That is how satan works. He is not usually frontal . . . he is tricky. He fools you with ostensibly good causes and lures you into his den.

Why was Jehoshaphat entangled with Ahab? Jehoshaphat was one of the godliest kings ever to reign in Judah, and Ahab was one of the most despicable snakes ever to coil on Israel's throne. Why did they get together?

The text does not give much of a clue (See 2 Chronicles 18:1), but we can surmise that due to Jehoshaphat's power, it was to Ahab's advantage to become allies. Ahab probably sought the alliance. Remember, Jehoshaphat was a nice person. In addition, he probably thought how good it would be to reunite the southern and northern kingdoms. Therefore, he gave his son in marriage to Ahab's daughter. It was for a good cause! Maybe the boy would have a positive influence on Athaliah and her mother, Jezebel! Sure!

A few years later, Jehoshaphat went down to Ahab's capital, Samaria. Ahab rolled out the red carpet. After they had stuffed themselves on Ahab's food, the crafty deceiver proposed a "spiritual" project to Jehoshaphat. "Will you go up with me against Ramoth-Gilead?" (See 2 Chronicles 18:3). Ramoth-Gilead was one of the cities of refuge ordained by God. It had fallen into the hands of the king of Syria. What could be more right than to go against this pagan king to recapture this city for the Lord and His people? Jehoshaphat pledged his allegiance to Ahab. It almost got him killed!

That is how satan ensnares believers. He is not up-front about the disastrous consequences of compromise with the world. He makes it look good. He makes it seem wholesome and even right.

Satan does not approach young women and ask, "Would you like to marry this drunken pagan bum who will abuse you and your children and make your life a living hell?" Instead, he presents you with a nice young man. He treats you right. He is just what you have always wanted, with one little exception. He is not a committed Christian. However, he attends church with you, and he has promised to let you raise the kids in the faith.

Satan does not walk up, pitchfork in hand, and ask with a diabolical grin, "How would you like to become a drunk or a dope addict? You will become a thief and a liar to support your habit, you will ruin your health, you will not be able to hold down a job, and you will shred your relationships with your family. Wanna sign up?"

Instead, he says, "Hey, you need to relax and feel good. You are under a lot of pressure. Your friends are all doing it. Do not spoil the fun. Smoke a joint, pop a pill, and take that drink!" Then, he ensnares you.

He does not come up and say, "How would you like to get a venereal disease or have a baby out of wedlock, or maybe kill one through abortion?" Or, "How would you like to destroy two families by committing adultery?" Rather, he says, "Sex is exciting! You are in love! How can it be wrong if it feels so right?"

That is how even godly people are lured into a compromise with the world; through subtlety. How does it work?

Notice how Jehoshaphat was sucked in deeper and deeper. First, he gave his son in marriage, probably for a good cause (to reunite the two kingdoms). Next, he accepted Ahab's hospitality, and foolishly gave his word about going into battle. At that point, his conscience was nagging him, and so he asked for a prophet so that they could inquire of the Lord. However, even after the godly Micaiah prophesied against Ahab's expedition, Jehoshaphat felt locked in. He had given his word. Therefore, he stood by while the godly prophet was hauled off to jail. His conscience must have been shouting at this point, but he had given his word!

Next, he naively agreed to Ahab's scheme where Jehoshaphat would wear his kingly robes into battle, while Ahab went incognito. Christians are generally trusting people. When they start running with the world, they are outsmarted very quickly! Jehoshaphat went into battle with the godless Ahab against the word of God's prophet. Except for God's grace, he would have been killed!

The subtlety of the world lures us and then we are locked in by forming wrong relationships that get us entangled even deeper. Jehoshaphat's experience reveals several areas where we as believers must be on guard against forming wrong relationships. The Bible is clear that it is a sin for a believer to enter a marriage with an unbeliever. *"Don't team up with those who are unbelievers. How can righteousness be a partner with wickedness? How can light live with darkness?"* (See 2 Corinthians 6:14; 1 Corinthians 7:39).

Most often, it seems to be a Christian girl who falls in love with a nice non-Christian guy and say that they have prayed about it and feel a peace that God will bring the man to Christ. Besides, if she drops him, she will not be able to witness to him! It is incredible how Christians will rationalize their disobedience even though it is going to plunge them into terrible heartache. It is never God's will for a Christian to marry a non-Christian. (If you are already married to an unbeliever, God's will is that you remain married and live a godly life – See 1 Corinthians 7:12-16.)

We must be aware of wrong *social* relationships. In this area, you must be very careful. If Jehoshaphat had not been there enjoying Ahab's hospitality, he would not have been so ready to join Ahab on his military expedition. It is not wrong and, in fact, it is right to form social relationships with unbelievers for leading them to faith in Christ. Jesus was a friend of sinners in that sense. However, you must be clear on your purpose, and you must not compromise your standards as a follower of Jesus Christ. *"Do not be deceived,"* Paul warns. *"Bad company corrupts good morals."* (See 1 Corinthians 15:33).

In Second Chronicles 19:2, we read, *"Should you help the wicked and love those who hate the Lord?"* Many Christians would answer, "Of course we should!" You had better read your Bible more carefully! It says that God hates the wicked (See Psalm 5:5) and that we should too (Psalm 139:20-22). You say, "Wait a minute, doesn't God love everyone, and aren't we supposed to love the sinner but hate the sin?" Suffice it to say here that the Bible is a bit more cautious and discerning than most Christians. Jude 23 says that on some, we are to *"have mercy with fear, hating even the garment polluted by the flesh."* You should not form primary friendships with unbelievers. Your closest friends must be those who share your values and goals in Christ.

What about wrong *spiritual* relationships? Jehoshaphat finds himself lined up with 400 false prophets against the lone prophet of God. How do you think Jehoshaphat felt as he watched this godly prophet boldly speak for God and then be hit in the face and be thrown in prison while Jehoshaphat marched off to battle on Ahab's side?

Christians say that Jesus said the world would know we are His disciples by our love and unity, so we need to bury our doctrinal differences and proclaim our unity and common ground. Certainly, Protestants are often divided over petty issues, and that is sin. Nevertheless, core theological issues mean the difference between heaven and hell. Some denominations are so spiritually corrupt that we cannot join with them in any cooperative sense without tarnishing the name of our Savior. "Love" that compromises cardinal truth is not biblical love.

We also need to be cautious about having wrong political relationships. Although our political system is not parallel to the situation in the text, there is a warning here for us as Christian citizens. As soon as Jehoshaphat entered into this military pact with Ahab, he lost his position of strength. Now he was committed to go into battle with a godless man who operated on different principles than he did. He had to work under Ahab's scheme in the battle. It almost cost him his life.

As believers, we may find it helpful at times to link up politically with unbelievers to achieve some common goal (such as pro-life or pro-family legislation). However, we need to think it through very carefully and keep our goals and methods clearly in view. Some Christians are being carried away with the political process, as if that is the answer to preserving our freedoms. While I am not disparaging our political responsibility as Christian citizens, I do maintain that the only hope for the world is the gospel. We dare not forget it! Wrong political relationships can suck us into a compromise with the world.

Another area to observe is wrong *business* relationships. Jehoshaphat did not learn his lesson with Ahab, and so he entered into a shipbuilding venture with Ahab's son, Ahaziah. The author pointedly states that this was a wicked deed on Jehoshaphat's part. The Lord judged him by destroying all the ships (See 2 Chronicles 20:35-37).

Many Christians never think of applying Second Corinthians 6:14, *"Do not be unequally yoked with unbelievers,"* to business ventures. However, the text does not stipulate marriage or any single area. It certainly applies to business relationships. If you get into a business partnership with an unbeliever, his goal is to make money, preferably as easily as possible. Your goal is to honor Christ (or it *should* be). You want to be honest and upright; he wants to cut corners if needs be. It will not work. You will end up compromising with the world.

If you were already in a business relationship with unbelievers when you came to Christ, then you need to give clear testimony to your partner of your new faith in Christ. In addition, you need to let him know that you plan now to obey God in your business, even if it means less profit. You may need to begin prayerfully planning a way out of the partnership. You especially need to be careful not to wrong any person in the way you get out of a wrong business alliance. It took time to get into the partnership, and it probably will take time to get out.

We have seen that compromise with the world is a great danger even for the most godly of believers. It is subtle, and it ensnares us through wrong relationships.

It may take time, but sin always has its consequences. Sometimes the consequences affect future generations more than our own. However, if you sow compromise with the world, you will not reap God's blessings. Jehoshaphat himself, apart from God's grace, would have lost his life in battle. He later did lose financially in his ungodly business alliance with Ahab's son.

Furthermore, Jehoshaphat's sin affected God's people. He did not say merely, "I am as you are," but also, "and my people as your people" (See 2 Chronicles 18:3). When Jehoshaphat went into war alongside Ahab, the army of Judah went with him, and no doubt, some lost their lives. Probably others in Judah would look at the godly Jehoshaphat's friendship with the evil Ahab and say, "There must not be much difference between Ahab's religion and ours. Surely, if there were any big difference, such a good man as Jehoshaphat wouldn't be so friendly with him." We never sin alone. Our sin always affects others in the body of Christ, especially the sins of a leader.

In addition, Jehoshaphat's sin helped the enemies of God in their wickedness (See 2 Chronicles 19:2). What if Ahab had won? Would he have fallen on his face before God? Hardly! He would have thanked his godless prophets and continued in his evil ways, thanks to Jehoshaphat. We never help sinners by compromising our standards to help them accomplish their purposes.

The decisive factor of this story is the devastating effect that Jehoshaphat's compromise with the world had on his children, grandchildren, great-grandchildren, and the entire southern kingdom. In chapters 21 and 22, we read that after Jehoshaphat's death, his son Jehoram (married to Athaliah) slaughtered all his brothers and then turned the nation to idolatry (See 2 Chronicles 21:6). God struck him with a terrible disease of the bowels, and he died after eight years in office. His son Ahaziah became king and lasted one year before he was murdered (See 2 Chronicles 22:3-4). Ahaziah's wicked mother, Athaliah, then slew all his sons (her own grandsons), except for Joash (a one-year-old) who was rescued and hidden from her. The Davidic kingly line from which Christ was descended came that close to being snuffed out. Then the wicked Athaliah ruled the land for six years. All this was the result of Jehoshaphat's compromise with the wicked Ahab.

Jehoshaphat fell to the trap of compromise, and he always had an excuse. It is amazing the number of excuses couples make to stay in a compromised relationship. *I'd rather settle for him than be alone.* What is wrong with being single? You are not alone (See Hebrews 13:5). If you are settling for an unhealthy relationship just to have a warm body near, you are missing the amazing indescribable intimacy God offers you. He will continue to politely step aside as you choose to accept less (See Psalm 25:16). Seek to be complete in Him (See Proverbs 8:17) first, and ditch this excuse before you miss "the one" that He has purposed for you to marry (See Psalm 139:16).

Here is another one: *I'm comfortable.* Is change something that makes you get embarrassed? Are you stringing a relationship along primarily because it has benefits, such as, money, companionship, image, physical intimacy, fun, familiar routine? Face it. We have all temporarily turned to everything from shopping to food for fulfillment. God offers to those who choose to trust in Him alone to meet all their needs (See Proverbs 3:5).

How about this one: *I love him.* If I had a dollar for every time I heard those words! Come on, man! I love my brother! I love my cat! There is a difference in loving and being "in love" and fully committed to the person you KNOW you were meant to marry . . . for better or worse. You have to get out of the "love" boat to walk on water. What I mean is, you have to move away from the one you "love" and walk out into the unknown toward God patiently until He brings you your one, true love. Do not miss your reward.

This one sounds convincing as to why you should stay together: *We've had sex.* Sex outside of marriage brings horrible consequences to every area of life. The Bible says, *"Flee from sexual immorality. All other sins a person commits are outside the body, but whoever sins sexually sins against his own body."* (1 Corinthians 6:18).

This one blinds people: *We have a child together.* You are single and pregnant, or maybe you are single with children already. You have a great reason to abandon, not your kids, but the bad relationship that entangles you (See Hebrews 12:1). Admit it. As children, many of us aspired to have better lives than those who raised us. Here is the kicker. Our starting point regarding relationships was the exact representation of what "mom" and "dad" modeled for each of us. It is better to stay single and model contentment and trust in the Lord than to marry, model a bad relationship, and end up having to raise your grandchildren who, according to statistics, will do the same. The choices YOU make affect future generations.

This one sounds good, but it is flawed: *I'm waiting until Mr. Right comes along.* If Mr. Right crosses your path, he will consider your low standards unattractive and immature. Your present relationship portrays evidence of the needy, insecure person you are choosing to be. The bad relationship you are in is a huge red flag to the Christ-like, confident mate you truly desire to be with.

This one keeps needy women bound: *We're engaged, already committed.* Have you agreed to marry him, but now you are having doubts? If there is doubt, DO NOT DO IT! Use the valuable opportunity you have now for a "time-out" to re-evaluate or choose to live the rest of your life with regret! "But," you say, "I've already started planning a wedding, and I'm looking forward to a honeymoon." Get your eyes off worldly things and ask God to open your spiritual eyes.

This one is common with those who are insecure or lack self-esteem: *I don't want to hurt his feelings.* Maybe you feel bad leaving him because he has spent so much time and money on you. Have you tried to walk away, but his craftiness persuaded you to stay? You are not a puppet; pull your heartstrings from his grip. Your people-pleasing nature, coupled with his controlling tendencies, is brewing up your worst nightmare. It is time to be concerned more with honoring God than your boyfriend.

This one is for the desperate heart: *He's "good" enough for me.* Maybe you are thinking, "I don't deserve any better," or perhaps you assume you would never land among the stars, so you have resolved never to shoot for the moon. Drop the measuring stick and pick up God's Word where "good enough" amounts to filthy rags for all of us. Our Father seeks to bless you, not because you deserve it, but because of His great love.

Finally, this one has caused many a difficult life of regret: *He'll change for the better!* Come on, who are you kidding? You cannot change him, and he is comfortable the way he is. You be who God called you to be and let God do the changing. Truthfully, you need to run the other direction. Bad relationships are poisonous.

A WORD OF THOUGHT

"Dear friends, if we deliberately continue sinning after we have received knowledge of the truth, there is no longer any sacrifice that will cover these sins." (Hebrews 10:26)

"If ye love me, obey my commandments." (John 14:15)

"And so, dear brothers and sisters, I plead with you to give your bodies to God because of all he has done for you. Let them be a living and holy sacrifice—the kind he will find acceptable. This is truly the way to worship him." (Romans 12:1)

"So fear the Lord and serve him wholeheartedly. Put away forever the idols your ancestors worshiped when they lived beyond the Euphrates River and in Egypt. Serve the Lord alone. But if you refuse to serve the Lord, then choose today whom you will serve. Would you prefer the gods your ancestors served beyond the Euphrates? Or will it be the gods of the Amorites in whose land you now live? But as for me and my family, we will serve the Lord." (Joshua 24:14-15)

"The man answered, 'You must love the Lord your God with all your heart, all your soul, all your strength, and all your mind.' And, 'Love your neighbor as yourself.'" (Luke 10:27)

"I say this because many deceivers have gone out into the world. They deny that Jesus Christ came in a real body. Such a person is a deceiver and an antichrist." (2 John 1:7)

"So put to death the sinful, earthly things lurking within

you. Have nothing to do with sexual immorality, impurity, lust, and evil desires. Don't be greedy, for a greedy person is an idolater, worshiping the things of this world." (Colossians 3:5)

8

THE FATHER HAS GIVEN YOU HIS KINGDOM

JESUS SAID, *"SEEK FIRST the Kingdom of God and His righteousness..."* (Matthew 6:33). When Jesus taught the disciples to pray, He did not tell them to pray for the *King* to come; He told them to pray for the *Kingdom* to come. For too long, "last day" teachings have simply tickled the people's ears and filled the teachers' bank accounts as they burden the people with certain events that are sure to happen, but they can never put a date, time, or place on these events.

When Jesus said we should seek first the kingdom of God, for instance, to whom was He speaking? When He zeroed in on the fears and weaknesses of those in His audience, those who worried about what they would wear or what they would eat, was He actually talking to an unnamed group in the future? Is the whole of the Sermon on the Mount a sermon for faithful Jews in attendance, for Christians living in the interim between Jesus' two advents, for both, or for neither? If it was for both, was it for both together or both separately?

To ask the question in terms of what the original audience must have heard is to answer the question. No one would have thought, "Well, this is all well and good for later. Jesus is talking about the church age, so when it starts, we will start to obey this command." No one would have thought, "This is for now, but when the church age begins, we will cease from seeking the kingdom and His righteousness." Certainly no one would have thought, "I will seek first His kingdom as a Jew until the church age begins. I will cease to pursue it during the church age. Then, I will pursue it again." The kingdom they were called to pursue, the kingdom we are called to pursue, is not now, and never has been, a divided kingdom. It is that kingdom, that one kingdom, where Christ reigns. It is that kingdom, that one kingdom, we enter through His righteousness alone. It is that kingdom, that one kingdom, where the one King meets all the needs of all God's people.

When we seek to divide the kingdom, we will inevitably end up seeking to divide the King. He is the King, after all, who so perfectly identifies with His people. Remember that when our King confronted that murderer of God's people named Saul, He demanded to know not why Saul was persecuting the citizens of the kingdom, but why Saul was persecuting Him. And when Saul was brought into that one kingdom as Paul, it was he who was changed, not the kingdom.

There is not now, nor were there ever, a kingdom on earth and a kingdom in heaven because there is only one King. We do not wait for His kingdom. We do not wait for His inauguration. All authority in heaven and on earth has been given to Him (See Matthew 28:18–20). Now He sits at the right hand of the Father (See Romans 8:34). Now He is bringing all things under subjection. Now He is conquering all His and our enemies (See 1 Corinthians 15:20–28). This is not merely a future hope but a present reality.

The good news is that our Lord reigns. This means that even when those over whom He rules try to divide themselves, try to draw sundry boundaries in the kingdom, they will always fail. We cannot tear asunder what God has brought together. This also means, however, that even those with multiple kingdoms, multiple peoples, and multiple epochs are His, just as I am. We are one because we confess one Lord, because we proclaim one faith, because we enjoy one baptism, because we serve one kingdom, because we love one King (See Ephesians 4:4–6).

His kingdom is not extending its boundaries. Wherever there is a there, there He reigns. It is, however, becoming more visible. The elect are being brought in. Knees in every nation are bowing. Tongues in every language are confessing. The Rock that was uncut by human hands, that destroyed the kingdoms of this world, is even now covering the earth as the waters cover the sea. This is the kingdom that we serve, the kingdom that has come, the kingdom that is forever. This is the one kingdom we all seek.

Just what is the kingdom of God—and when does it appear? Is it *in heaven*? Is it the *universal church*? Is it a denomination? Is it the *Millennium*? Is it "in the *hearts of men*" or merely the "*good within* each person"? Millions believe these popular ideas—yet their interpretations are often based upon faulty premises, preconceived assumptions, inconsistent doctrines, flawed and unchallenged religion, and biased traditions. The bottom line, they are ALL wrong! Unnecessary confusion and disagreement reign. Let us accurately explore the topic of the kingdom throughout the Scriptures and find unity and clarity on this important and crucial topic.

Only a few verses later, in the same chapter, Christ

stated, "But seek you *first* the kingdom (government) of God, and His righteousness; and all these things shall be added unto you" (vs. 33). Christians must be continually seeking the kingdom (government) of God *FIRST*—above everything else—in their lives! How can they do this if they do not know *what* it is—when it will come—or how it affects their own salvation?

The Bible teaches that the kingdom (*government*) of God rules over the people and nations of the earth. The nations are not actually part of the kingdom, any more than the average citizen of any country is part of the government that rules over them. One must enter the kingdom (government) of God to be in it. Therefore, we must ask, as distinct from those who are governed by it, which is actually in the kingdom?

In First Corinthians 15:50-51, Paul stated, "Now this I say, brethren, that *flesh and blood cannot inherit the kingdom* of God; neither does corruption inherit incorruption. Behold, I show you a *mystery*…" Certainly, this *is* a mystery to almost everyone—that flesh and blood human beings cannot enter the kingdom of God. It would be helpful to read the entirety of this "resurrection chapter" of First Corinthians 15.

Do you see, then, how no *church* can possibly be the kingdom of God? Churches are physical. Flesh and blood physical people are able to enter and exit a church building. So, this rules out all churches from being the kingdom (government) of God.

The kingdom of God cannot include flesh and blood people!

There have been numerous attempts to find the key concept, which unifies the whole of the Scriptures. In conservative Christian circles, most scholars opt for either the covenant or the Kingdom of God as that unifying theme.

The covenant is the term used to describe the legal agreement that God has made and renewed with mankind from the time of Adam up till the present gospel era. The primary covenant agreement is that made with Abraham, a promise of sovereign grace appropriated through grace, while the most detailed example of the agreement is found in God's renewal of the covenant with the people of Israel at Mt. Sinai.

The form of the Sinai agreement follows the typical legal arrangement made between a king and his vassal state. Two copies of the agreement would be made, one held by the king and the other kept by the vassal power. They would usually keep the document at their religious shrine. In Israel's case, Moses had two copies of the Ten Commandments, one for Jehovah, and the other for Israel. Both copies were kept safe in the Ark: the wooden box or throne upon which the Lord sat when His Shekinah glory entered the Holy of Holies in the Tabernacle. The content of the Sinai covenant was simple enough, although its details were quite extensive. The books of Numbers, Deuteronomy, and Leviticus set out the covenant in detail. In it, the Lord notes that He is their God, and they are His people. He details all that He has done for them - brought them out of Egypt with a mighty and powerful arm (saved them). He sets out what He intends to do for His people (the blessings), details obligations, and the consequences of rebellion (cursing). The actual Ten Commandments are a shorthand version of the covenant details, and of course, the New Testament, or New Covenant of the gospel era, follows much the same form.

In simple terms, the Sinai covenant reaffirms the Abrahamic covenant, namely the promise of divine grace and this appropriated through faith. The Law, of course, gives shape to the fruit of faith, while at the same time forcing dependence on faith, rather than works, for the appropriation of the promised blessings of the covenant.

Yet, although the covenant is such a dominant theme in the scriptures, it is not so much the agreement itself, which dominates, but rather the divine grace which the agreement promises. The content primarily concerns the promise of a kingdom. The Bible is the story of a kingdom lost and of God's promised intention and active intervention to re-establish that kingdom, and that in a far grander way. This then is the unifying concept of the scriptures.

A kingdom, as we all know, is a defined area containing a subject people, ruled by a lord or king, who defines the laws of the land and blesses all who faithfully serve him.

The Kingdom of God (or Kingdom of Heaven as Matthew likes to call it) is similar to an earthly kingdom. God as King and Lord rules over His people, subject to His commands, and blesses them out of His gracious mercy. As we experience the Kingdom today, and as we will experience it in the age to come, we are actually entering into a promise made long ago. "I will be your God and you will be my people." (See Leviticus 26:3-13). In fact, it is the promised experience of the Garden of Eden, yet even now, and certainly in the age to come, it will be a far grander reality. The Kingdom is the assembling of all God's people under His rule and care, experiencing complete unity and oneness with each other and the Lord God. God is present, the people seeing Him face to face, knowing Him intimately as well as knowing each other in the same way. The Kingdom is the dimension in which we find God, each other, and ourselves. It is the ultimate community of fellowship and love.

Throughout history, it has been possible for humanity to enter into the Kingdom of God, into the community of God's children. Those who have entered have (partly) experienced the blessings of membership, for God keeps His covenant, His agreement, and His Word. They have come to know God. They have found peace (See 1 John 1:3, Ephesians 2, Hebrews 12). Yet, the ultimate reality of the Kingdom has always awaited a future consummation. So today, as with the saints of old, we wait for the dawning of heaven, of the picture of Revelation 21-22. Of most importance, we rely on the promise of Scripture that those who experience the Kingdom in the present will be full members in the age to come; they will participate fully in the blessings of heaven (See John 5:24).

What will the Heavenly Kingdom be like? Attempting to visualize such a dimension is quite beyond us. It is more than we could ever imagine. The Bible gives us a few hints, but that is about all. It seems that the Kingdom of Heaven is going to be a new community, a community or society which, when established, will hail the glory of God. It will not just exist for resurrected humans, but it will exist as a united whole of the created order - Angels, Powers, and Authorities. The Kingdom of God will infuse the whole cosmos, and peace shall reign into the eons of all ages. The most marvelous truth is this: we mere humans, under Jesus, will rule over it all (See Matthew 19:30, 1 Corinthians

6:2,3).

It would be nice to know why God is creating this glorious Kingdom, this new community of love. Yet, the Scriptures say little on the matter, and so we are left with conjecture. A similar question concerns His reasons for creating the earth, especially given God's foreknowledge of our rebellion and the subsequent need for Jesus to die. Again, this question leads to our place and purpose in the grand scheme of it all. What indeed is the purpose of a believer's life? Life's purpose is usually put in the terms, "To tell others about Jesus and so gather a people unto the Lord." There is little doubt that we should make the good news of the gospel known in our world, but is this the purpose of our life? Why does God need to use such a rebellious group of servants for a task He could well do Himself? Why bother creating us in the first place, given the inevitable outcome?

No, life has more to do with preparing us for our place in the Kingdom, preparing us to rule with Christ. The center of it has to do with God's determined will to gather a people to Himself, a new creation, a Kingdom of priests. Why He determines to do this, we really do not know. Is it just His character of love? What does matter is that God is shaping an eternal Kingdom, and in Christ, we are part of it.

So, for us today, the nature of the Kingdom of God is that of a community of believers bound under the rule of Christ and blessed through the indwelling presence of the Holy Spirit, a people gathered with God, ruled by Him, blessed by Him. At this moment in time, we await the coming of the Kingdom in its final glorious manifestation at the return of Christ. We await the dawning of the eternal heavenly society.

The whole movement of the Bible is the record of God setting up a simple expression of His Kingdom in the Garden of Eden, of the destruction of that Kingdom and of God's step-by-step re-establishment of the Kingdom in a far greater form, which in its fullness, for us, is still future.

There have been numerous manifestations of the Kingdom of God throughout human history. In fact, every time God's rule is established in the life of any group of people, any family, or indeed in the life of an individual person, there and then a manifestation of the Kingdom of God becomes a reality. This manifestation, this realization of the Kingdom, is fully and completely the Kingdom of God on earth. Not only does it image the heavenly reality of the Kingdom for which we await, but it is also for that moment the Kingdom. Being members of that Kingdom guarantees membership of the Kingdom in the age to come.

The Scriptures record the establishment of a number of manifestations of the Kingdom. Each Kingdom, which God has established within human history, has, with ever-increasing clarity, imaged the Heavenly Kingdom of God. In that sense, each has served to reveal to humankind, through an unfolding revelation, God's plan to establish a Kingdom through which He unites all things to Himself.

This does not mean that these Kingdoms are merely bare representations to show us what is to come. For that moment in time for which they exist, they are the real thing. What happens is that the future reality of the Heavenly Kingdom bursts into our earthly dimension in a way we can perceive and understand, and yet in a way that points beyond itself to something greater. So, therefore, those who are in it are in the Kingdom. They are in the Kingdom for that moment and for the infinite future.

What we need to do now is examine the different modes of the Kingdom of God, the different ways in which the fellowship, the community, the society of God's children, have emerged within human history.

At the beginning, God formed a simple expression of His Kingdom. He made a people in His image where relationships were possible. He ruled those subject to Him, and He blessed them, especially with the blessing of His friendship. Adam and Eve walked with God in the garden of Eden (See Genesis 3:8). Yet, what they had was lost through their rebellion. In the human family, there were many "great ones," but finally, judgment came in the flood.

The Lord God saved a people to Himself through the surging waters of the flood. Noah and his family shared in the Post-Flood Kingdom of God. Under the promised blessing of the rainbow, they lived as a people bound under the rule of God. Yet, sin continued to affect the Kingdom, and finally, at Babel, the people rose up against God's rule and so were scattered.

Abram, along with his family, left Ur for the promised land. He was called by the living God and promised a Kingdom. Following a harsh journey and a time of struggle in Canaan, his family, under the living God, began to possess the promised Kingdom. Yet it was a minute realization of the promise, with his family ending up as slaves in Egypt.

With a mighty and outstretched arm, the Lord led His people out of slavery. Following their struggle to possess the land of Canaan, the Kingdom came to fruition in the nation of Israel. In its institutions, the coming Kingdom was prefigured in a tangible way (See 1 Kings 10). So, the people lived in their city of God where He was pleased to dwell (See 1 Chronicles 23:25), ruled by their king who represented the rule of God (See Deuteronomy 17:14-20) and through the priestly office came close to Him. Yet, failure again beset the Kingdom, a failure that ended in the destruction of the nation by the Babylonians.

During the time of the Historic Kingdom, while it was beset with failure, prophets were raised up by the living God to comment on what was happening. On the surface, they spoke to the people of their day and encouraged them to turn from their rebellion and to live again for the Lord. They warned the people that continued rebellion would result in the destruction of the nation of Israel. Following the lead of the popular prophets, the people saw the Kingdom of Israel as eternal and safe in the hands of the Lord. Few, therefore, responded to the bleak words of the prophets of the Lord. Slowly the prophets revealed that the Kingdom of Israel was but an image of a coming Kingdom whose glory would outshine all the institutions of the nation, even the glory of Solomon's reign. They pictured something quite beyond the earthly reality they had already experienced, although similar in form, i.e., Ezekiel's New Temple.

When the people of Israel returned from exile in Babylon, they certainly expected that the Kingdom they were about to set up would be the real thing. The prophecies of Haggai and Zechariah rightly convinced them to establish a representative expression of the Kingdom for that moment in history. Yet, very soon, the people saw that the Kingdom, which was unfolding before their very eyes, shared little of the glory of the Historic

Kingdom of their forefathers. At the completion of the Temple, some of those who had known the glory of Solomon's temple actually cried at the sight of their own meager efforts. In the end, what eventuated was a poor imitation of the Historic Kingdom. The people soon began to realize that the words of Haggai and Zechariah had more to say about a coming Kingdom than the limited attempts at Jewish nationalism, which was to come to an end in 70 AD. None-the-less, there was set in motion a driving expectation in the Jewish people for a Davidic Messiah who would establish a Kingdom in power.

When Jesus appeared in Palestine, He announced, "The Kingdom is at hand" (See Mark 1:15). It is about to burst into history. Although the Jews were waiting for the coming Kingdom, they were unable to align Jesus with the expected mighty Davidic Messiah. Even John the Baptist was confused (See Luke 7:18-23). Jesus pinpointed the problem when he said, "My Kingdom is not of this world' (See John 18:36). Only those who have their eyes opened can see Jesus' messianic role and the Kingdom at hand.

It was after Jesus had fulfilled His messianic role, particularly His crucifixion, that the Kingdom came in its present spiritual dimension. The actual moment in time was at Pentecost when the Spirit was poured out upon the disciples gathered together in the upper room at Jerusalem. This was the point of Peter's sermon to the crowd that had gathered to watch the strange behavior of the disciples. What Joel had prophesied concerning the outpouring of God's Spirit as the heralding sign of the coming of the new age was now being fulfilled in the sight of all. The Kingdom has come (See Acts 2:14-42).

For us then, as members of the Present Kingdom,

Christ is at this moment ruling a people gathered about Him (See Acts 2:36). He is protecting us like a city wall (See Hebrews 13:6). He is mediating between us and the Father as our great High Priest (See Hebrews 9:24), and we as a temple are indwelt by His Spirit (See Ephesians 2:21-22).

Although the Present Kingdom is in a sense spiritual rather than physical or tangible, it does become localized and visible in the church. For it is here where two or three gather in the name of Christ, centered on His presence (See Matthew 18:20) that the reality of the Kingdom becomes visible. Here, at a localized point in time and space, a people gather as they will gather on the last day. In fact, there is a sense where the gathering is actually the gathering on that last day. It is as if we are actualizing the reality of our place before the throne of the living God; it is as if we are there now. As the children of God confront their living God, they worship Him, they bow before Him, and adore Him. Then, from that confrontation, they experience friendship with God and with each other—they commune; they become the body of Christ, one with Him, bound in love (See Ephesians 2:16, 19, 3:6, 4:3-4, 25, 5:21-33).

Although the organization or the institution of the church is not the Kingdom, the gathering of God's people is certainly a visible manifestation of the Kingdom in the here and now. The root meaning of "church" in the Greek is "assembly" or "gathering." There are many assemblies other than a Christian one (See Acts 19:32). The church we are concerned with is the assembly around God, and it is this for which we await. Yet, in a sense, we are even now gathered with Christ in the heavenlies (See Ephesians 2:6), for where He is, there will His servants be also (See John

12:26). The reality of this gathering is made real to us through the Spirit, for where two or three are gathered together, there is Christ in the midst (See Matthew 18:20), and so we are to exhort each other not to forsake the gathering together of the brotherhood (See Hebrews 10:24-25). So, the primary substance of the Kingdom is the gathering of a people unto the Lord, a community, a new society, a fellowship of love and unity. This people gather subject to God's Word, blessed by His presence. Such is the nature of the church.

The Present Kingdom, and its visible expression in the church, is in itself a foretaste of the Kingdom to come (See Ephesians 1:10). We, as God's children, await the return of Christ to bring in that Kingdom in all its fullness. We wait for all things to be made subject to Christ so that in that coming day we may gather in the heavenlies before our father God (See Revelation 21:3, 22:3-5). It is then, with Christ, we will begin our task as a new creation, to rule the cosmos, to bring light to darkness, that all may be united under the one head, even Christ.

In the New Testament, the different modes of the Kingdom may be represented as a present reality experienced in the Christian church and as a coming future heavenly reality. The present reality is a fading reality as the church moves toward *the great falling away*, the tribulation and the coming of "the new heaven and the new earth."

John the Baptist burst into Palestine with the message that God is about to act to release his people, to secure the victory, and set up the Kingdom through the work of the long expected Messiah. A great expectancy develops, but the people look toward to the political sphere instead of the spiritual. The Kingdom established by Jesus is not of this order of things and therefore is not easily seen.

In a quite unexpected way, the preliminary events that lead up to the establishment of the Kingdom is fleshed out in the life of Jesus Himself. He, representing the new Israel, enters the sea at His baptism. He stands the test in the wilderness for forty days and forty nights. He struggles against the enemy, bringing ruin to his cities (See Matthew 12:25-29). Finally, He is victorious over the enemy on the cross (See 1 Corinthians 15:55-57). It turns out that the Messiah, the suffering Servant, is a corporate identity; He represents the people of Israel, the children of God. Unlike faithless Israel, always rebellious, Jesus is the faithful servant of God; He does not fail the test. The glorious truth is that we, in all our frailty, can identify with the Messiah; we can stand in His shadow, join in His journey, and share in His victory (See Philippians 3:10).

At Pentecost, the Spirit is poured out, and God's people share in the blessing of knowing Him as Father (See Romans 8:15, Galatians 4:6). The Kingdom, in which Jesus is Prophet, Priest, and King, has finally come for us to dwell in. Yet, even the Kingdom's coming in this spiritual mode is not the final reality; this Kingdom too will fade. Trouble will beset the church, and finally, all will be shattered in the great and terrible tribulation. Yet in that day, when all melt away at the return of Christ, a new Kingdom will dawn—eternity will be ours (See Matthew 24:9-14).

Although we are members of the Present Kingdom at this moment, we are also part of the preliminary events, which are even now moving inexorably toward the establishment of the future Heavenly Kingdom. In Christ, the initial events have already been fulfilled, and so we await the great and final battle heralding Christ's return and the establishment of the Kingdom in glory.

The sequence of events began with Jesus' death on the cross. Here the captives were released from their bondage to sin and death. Jesus achieved on the cross an "Exodus" for His brothers (See Luke 9:31). Then in the wilderness of Galilee, He meets with His disciples and teaches them, and on the mountain, in glory, He leaves them. Following Pentecost, like Joshua of old, the Spirit of Jesus leads His people into battle against the powers of darkness. So at this present moment, we struggle, "not against flesh and blood, but against the rulers, against the authorities, against the powers of this dark world and against the spiritual forces of evil in the heavenly realms." (Ephesians 6:12). Soon Jesus will return to work the final victory over satan. The dead in Christ will rise, a legion to stand with Christ in the heavenlies. Then shall the new heavens and new earth unfold, and all principalities and powers in the cosmos will kneel before Christ, the King, and then will He hand over the Kingdom to the Father, perfected (See 1 Corinthians 15:28).

There is a sense where we find ourselves in two places. As members of the Present Kingdom, we experience the blessings of Christ's indwelling, particularly when two or three gather. We experience faith, hope, and love. Yet, we also experience the limitations of the present moment, of compromise or failure. We experience chastisement and the disciplining of the Lord. All about us fades, and so our eyes look upward to the coming age of glory. As members of an army striving to bring in the Heavenly Kingdom, we experience the times of testing and trial, of pain and suffering, of struggle. We do know pain, we do experience trouble, but we also taste victory. Therefore, in this present moment, we are in the Kingdom and at the same time awaiting its final manifestation.

Generally speaking, within the preliminary events of the Heavenly Kingdom, we find ourselves in the struggle period. As such, we can identify easily with the books of Genesis, Joshua, Judges, First and Second Samuel, Ezra and Nehemiah. Yet, it is also true that we, as a group or as individuals, are able at times to identify very readily with the period of test and trial. In our personal lives, or in the life of our church, we can find ourselves at different points in the journey toward the Promised Land. Thus books such as Exodus and Numbers are also very relevant for the disciple today. So then, we find ourselves within the Kingdom, experiencing the blessings, but also the discipline of the Lord. We also find ourselves in the lead-up to the Kingdom's establishment, experiencing salvation, test and trial, struggle and victory. We straddle life as members of the Kingdom while struggling to bring it in.

The Present Kingdom is overlapped by the Heavenly Kingdom; the *now / not yet* reality of the Kingdom of God. It is not hard to conceive of the Kingdom of God as an entity presently inaugurated and experienced both spiritually and physically in the church. As members of the Present Kingdom, we await the day of the kingdom's final realization in the Heavenly Kingdom. Yet, the Kingdom is far too dynamic to be confined to a time-line. In our experience, the Kingdom is *not yet* - it is inaugurated, but not realized. Yet, from God's perspective, the Kingdom is already realized; it is *now*. The Son of Man has come with that great throng of the redeemed to the Ancient of Days, is upon His throne, and all knees bow before Him (See Daniel 7:13-14). As Paul says, *"God raised us up with Christ and seated us with him in the heavenly realms in Christ Jesus."* (Ephesians 2:6).

A WORD OF THOUGHT

"Dear friends, if we deliberately continue sinning after we have received knowledge of the truth, there is no longer any sacrifice that will cover these sins." (Hebrews 10:26)

Jesus answered, "My Kingdom is not an earthly kingdom. If it were, my followers would fight to keep me from being handed over to the Jewish leaders. But my Kingdom is not of this world." (John 18:36)

"May your Kingdom come soon. May your will be done on earth, as it is in heaven." (Matthew 6:10)

"You won't be able to say, 'Here it is!' or 'It's over there!' For the Kingdom of God is already among you." (Luke 17:21)

But if I am casting out demons by the power of God, then the Kingdom of God has arrived among you. (Luke 11:20)

He replied, "You are permitted to understand the secrets of the Kingdom of God. But I use parables to teach the others so that the Scriptures might be fulfilled: When they look, they won't really see. When they hear, they won't understand.'" (Luke 8:10)

9

GOD'S ADOPTION PLAN

IT IS GOOD NEWS WHEN JESUS tells us in John's gospel that "I will not leave you orphaned; I am coming to you" (John 14:18). Through the Spirit, we can be united to Jesus Christ, becoming daughters and sons of God through our union with the one perfect Son of God.

This image of adoption is a central image for Paul in speaking about this life of salvation in Christ and the new identity that we enter into in Christ. On the one hand, the Spirit assures Christians that they already belong to God—as ones united to Jesus Christ, they can cry out to God as Father. Yet, as Paul indicates later in the same chapter, this adoption is also a future reality for which "the creation waits with eager longing for the revealing of the children of God" (Romans 8:19). For "not only the creation, but we ourselves, who have the first fruits of the Spirit, groan inwardly while we wait for adoption, the redemption of our bodies" (Romans 8:23). We are adopted children of God, able to pray to the Father by the Spirit. Yet even this is a foretaste of the consummation of adoption for which the creation groans and waits

While Paul's metaphor of adoption begins as a legal act, it does not end there. It ends with membership in the household of God (See Ephesians 2:19; Galatians 6:10) and a calling to live the reality of this new identity. God's legal act of adopting children into His family also results in an eschatological conditioned identity. When we are given an identity in Christ, we are called to live it. For example, the doxological opening of Ephesians 1 says that God "destined us for adoption as his children through Jesus Christ" (Ephesians 1:5). As the blessings of being in Christ are unfolded in the following verses, Paul returns to the language of adoption and inheritance. "In Christ we have also obtained an inheritance having been destined according to the purpose of him who accomplishes all things according to his counsel and will, so that we, who were the first to set our hope on Christ, might live for the praise of his glory" (Ephesians 1:11–12, emphasis added). We are called to reflect the behavior of our new identity: as those who have been conferred a new adopted identity in Christ and who therefore seek to live in this glorious inheritance from God.

Yet one cannot become an adopted child of God by trying hard to be one—by exercising spiritual disciplines, by giving to the poor, or by loving one's neighbor. Instead, these acts are the fruit of God's act of adopting us, the result of God bringing us into a strange new world: as believers, God has united us to Christ and has given us His Spirit, which empowers us to serve the Father in cheerful gratitude. We belong to the household of God. Ephesians 2:10–22 explores the astonishing implications of God establishing this household in Christ, of creating a "new humanity."

Gentiles were once "strangers to the covenants of promise." However, "now in Christ Jesus you who once were far off have been brought near by the blood of

Christ." For Christ "is our peace; in his flesh he has made both groups into one and has broken down the dividing wall, that is, the hostility between us. He has abolished the law with its commandments and ordinances, that he might create in himself one new humanity in place of the two, thus making peace, and might reconcile both groups to God in one body through the cross, thus putting to death that hostility through it" (Ephesians 2:13–16).

We are adopted children who share in this "one new humanity" in Christ. Truly, we have been adopted into this family and are called to live as children of God, united in family fellowship with those whose skin color and culture are different from our own. God created this new humanity. We did not. But we have been graciously incorporated into it. We are already adopted children of God, even though—as sinners—we act as if we belong to ourselves. God's people, the church, do not yet reflect the full glory of their adopted identity.

Galatians 4:4-5 teaches us that at the perfect time—God's time—the Father sent the Son to be the Savior of the world. He did this "so that He might redeem those who were under the Law, that we might receive the adoption as sons." The sacrifice of the Lord Jesus on the cross for our sins was fully accepted by the Father as the demands of His righteous law were fully met. As a result, those who find refuge from the condemnation of the Law in the "accepted One" find themselves fully accepted by the Heavenly Father as members of His cherished family.

Christians are legally adopted as sons into God's family. Paul uses the term 'adopted as sons' to write to the believers in Rome, where they would have understood this in a specific context. Now, in the Jewish culture of the Old

Testament, people did not practice adoption, generally speaking. Why? Because they had other ways of dealing with this problem. One way was called levirate marriage. This meant a brother was to marry his brother's widow and raise children for his brother. Another alternative was polygamy. In First Samuel, Elkanah's first wife, Hannah, was "without child" - that is, not able to bear children and so Elkanah married another wife in order to have children. The third alternative used sometimes was easy divorce. So, generally speaking, levirate marriage, polygamy, and easy divorce solved the problem of adoption in the Old Testament Jewish culture.

Now in the Roman and Greek cultures, adoption was widely practiced. Normally it meant the adoption of young males, not females. The adoptee, usually a young male, was taken out of his previous state and installed, or placed, in a new relationship with his new father. In a Roman household, the father was the potentate, the person of great power, who could even kill members of his own family, although this was not often practiced. So the Greek word for adoption is *huiothesia* - *huios* means son, and *thesia* means placement. It means the installation of a person as a son. All his old debts were canceled, and in effect, the adopted child started a new life with new privileges and responsibilities under the rule of the new father.

"But when the right time came, God sent his Son, born of a woman, subject to the law. God sent him to buy freedom for us who were slaves to the law, so that he could adopt us as his very own children. And because we are his children, God has sent the Spirit of his Son into our hearts, prompting us to call out, "Abba, Father." Now you are no longer a slave but God's own child. And since you are his child, God has made you his heir." (Galatians 4:4-7).

Adoption is a legal act of God on our behalf, in the same way as justification. Justification is a legal language in Scripture. We stand before the judgment bar of God as hopeless sinners, condemned to death, with nothing to offer for our own redemption. But Christ comes and stands before His Father at the judgment bar and offers His perfect righteousness, His full atonement for our sins, and His perfect keeping of God's law as our substitute. And so God the Father declares us not guilty, not because we paid the penalty. Not because we have a righteousness of our own. Only because of the perfect and complete work of His Son Jesus Christ on our behalf. And so, legally, we stand before God clothed in the righteousness of Christ.

In the same way, adoption is a legal language in Scripture. We see this in the passage we just read in Galatians. Notice chapter four, verses four and five: "But when the fullness of time had come, God sent forth His Son, born of a woman, born under the law, to redeem those who were under the law, that we might receive the adoption as sons."

Note that we are adopted as sons, and we need to be very careful here to say what Scripture actually says and to understand why it says it. Today, many people want us to use so-called gender-neutral versions of the Bible that remove all the masculine and feminine references. That may be politically correct in some circles, but it is not Biblically correct. We must completely reject that kind of thinking.

And here, in this passage, we have one of the strongest arguments. The wording here is clearly masculine. The word is *huiothesia*. It means, literally, "to be placed as a son." And in Galatians 4:4 the word is translated "the adoption of sons." The word is clearly masculine. Not merely adoption as children, not as sons and daughters, but adoption as sons. Yes, God created us male and female. But as it concerns our redemption, we who are in Christ, men and women and boys and girls alike, are adopted by God as sons, in that sense, as Paul says, "there is neither male nor female."

Why is that important? We need to remember that Paul is writing to people who were under the rule of the Roman Empire. They were subject to Roman law. Although we do see forms of adoption practiced in the Old Testament, there was no mention of precisely this kind of adoption in the Mosaic law. The picture that Paul, by the Holy Spirit, is using here in Galatians is definitely the Roman law of adoption of sons because that is what the people who received this letter would have understood.

And adoption as a son in Roman law was something very specific. Adoption as a son in Roman law meant that you had the right to the name and the citizenship of the person who adopted you and the right to inherit his property. The adopted son had the same rights and privileges as a naturally born son. These were rights that were not granted to an adopted daughter and the law also granted the one who adopted that son the full rights and responsibilities of a father, full authority over the adopted son, and full responsibility to care for him. There is a bestowment of *exousia* – authority, so that you can come to the presence of God without fear and without shame, without embarrassment. You know that you have the right to come to His presence because God has given you the right to come. And then, this is what adoption is all about—

you are children of God.

And we read the same thing in Romans chapter three, verses 23 to 25, "For all have sinned and fall short of the glory of God, being justified freely by His grace through the redemption that is in Christ Jesus, whom God set forth as a propitiation by His blood, through faith." (KJV).

So we are justified by the redemption that is in Christ Jesus, and we are also adopted by the redemption that is in Christ Jesus. The one transaction, redeeming us, buying us out of the slave market of sin, which is the picture here that one transaction between God, the Son, and God, the Father, has wrought both legal acts on our behalf: justification and adoption. Not only have we been declared not guilty by God, the Judge, but God, the Judge, has adopted us as His own sons!

What a turnabout! We were on our way to hell. We were without God, without hope in the world. Lost, spiritually dead. Totally unable to save ourselves. Filthy with sin. Guilty through and through. We were condemned to eternal death. The righteous Judge has pronounced the sentence against us according to His perfect Law, and all that awaited was for us to be cast into hell.

But then, God's only begotten Son comes, and in one great transaction, He not only causes the Judge who condemns us to declare us not guilty, but He also causes the Judge who had condemned us to adopt us as His own sons! What indescribable grace! What infinite mercy! The Apostle John marvels at it in his first epistle. "Behold what manner of love the Father has bestowed on us, that we should be called the sons of God!" (1 John 3:1). Unbelievable. We could not believe it was possibly true if God's Word did not tell us that it is so.

"Behold, what manner of love" John says. Behold! Comprehend the meaning of it! Understand what has been done for you! Rejoice in it! Glory in it! Rest in it! Live in it! God, your condemning Judge, is now God, your loving Father!

For us, this means that we have been given the name of Christ and have the right to be called Christians. Our inheritance is nothing less than the property of our Heavenly Father—all the spiritual riches that are in Christ, both in the present life and in our life to come.

The adopted son also had the right to the father's citizenship of the Empire. We also obtained a new citizenship when our Father adopted us, and we have become citizens of heaven—our true home.

The father who adopts was also granted full rights and responsibilities of a natural father—he had complete authority over the adopted son and also had the legal role of caregiver. With full, loving authority over us, our Father has accepted His responsibility to care for us, and He also has the right, and desire, to correct us when we are wrong and to discipline us when we step out of line.

Ephesians 1:13-14 teaches us that at the moment we believed the gospel, we were sealed in Christ "with the Holy Spirit of promise, who is given as a pledge of our inheritance, with a view to the redemption of God's own possession, to the praise of His glory." The Holy Spirit, who right now indwells us, is God's down-payment on His own promise. As fully mature adopted sons, we are the rightful heirs, in Christ, of an unspeakable inheritance. The Holy Spirit's presence is proof.

Our adoption by God also changes our relationship with every person in the world—both Christians and non-

Christians. Our relationship to everyone else who has been adopted by God is changed, and no matter what the distance is between us—whether they live near or far, or whether they are alive today or have already fallen asleep and passed on from this life, they are all our brothers and sisters.

Our relationship with non-believers has also changed, for they are still dead in their sins, and we are no longer a part of their family. We have different interests from them; now, our interests are no longer selfish and centered on the glorifying of ourselves or of other people, but we should only be concerned with bringing glory to God.

Our Father God is infinitely patient, wise, and loving, and the Bible tells us that the fact that God does discipline us is proof in itself that we have been adopted into His family. Ephesians 2:3 teaches us that before we were regenerated by the Holy Spirit and faith came from the hearing of the gospel (See Romans 10:17), we were "children of wrath." Now, according to First John 3:2, "we are children of God." No longer are we "children of the devil" (See 1 John 3:10), but fully accepted and adopted sons and daughters of the King of kings. We belong to Him. We belong in His family.

We have a new relationship with God—through believing in what Jesus Christ has done for us. God, the Judge, who must punish every sin we have ever committed according to the just and perfect law, has instead become our loving Father who forgives us.

God is no longer far off and unapproachable, but near and easily accessible; we can come to Him whenever we desire through the intercession of Christ. The Bible tells us that God wants us to come to Him; He longs for us to spend time with Him, to talk with Him about everything that is happening in our lives—our Father in heaven wants to listen to us and care for us.

God is your Father!

A WORD OF THOUGHT

"God decided in advance to adopt us into his own family by bringing us to himself through Jesus Christ. This is what he wanted to do, and it gave him great pleasure." (Ephesians 1:5)

"This means that Abraham's physical descendants are not necessarily children of God. Only the children of the promise are considered to be Abraham's children." (Romans 9:8)

"So you have not received a spirit that makes you fearful slaves. Instead, you received God's Spirit when he adopted you as his own children. Now we call him, 'Abba, Father.'" (Romans 8:15)

"And now that you belong to Christ, you are the true children of Abraham. You are his heirs, and God's promise to Abraham belongs to you." (Galatians 3:29)

"For all who are led by the Spirit of God are children of God." (Romans 8:14)

www.ingramcontent.com/pod-product-compliance
Lightning Source LLC
Chambersburg PA
CBHW071455070526
44578CB00001B/352